Bloodstains in Ulster

Bloodstains in Ulster

The Notorious Case of Robert the Painter

Tom McAlindon

The Liffey Press

Published by
The Liffey Press
Ashbrook House, 10 Main Street,
Raheny, Dublin 5, Ireland
www.theliffeypress.com

© 2006 Tom McAlindon

A catalogue record of this book is
available from the British Library.

ISBN 1-904148-91-3

Printed in the Republic of Ireland by ColourBooks Ltd.

About the Author

Tom McAlindon was born and grew up in Belfast and was in his late teens at the time of the Taylor case. He was educated at St Malachy's College, Belfast, University College Cork, and Cambridge University. He has lived and worked in England and elsewhere since 1957 and is currently Emeritus Professor of English at the University of Hull.

Acknowledgements, Sources, Method

For information and advice I am indebted to the following: Alex Ashe, the Gibbons family (this name has been changed), Terence Donaghy, Gerald Dowd, Patrick and Brendan Cassidy, Pascal O'Hare, Colette Hamill (née Casey), Rosaleen Murphy (née Casey), Nancy and Michael Sherry, Archie Williamson, James Kelly, John Cole, Eric Kaufmann and Hugh Jordan. I am especially indebted to Kathleen Woodhouse (née McGowan).

The bulk of the legal material in the book I have derived from the very full accounts of the two Taylor trials and the Taylor appeal given in *The Irish News*, from shorter notices in *The Belfast Telegraph*, *The News-Letter* and *The Northern Whig*, and from records found in *The Northern Ireland Law Reports*, *The Northern Ireland Legal Quarterly* and the Public Records Office of Northern Ireland. All other facts and details of substantive importance have been derived from communications with individuals who were close in one way or another to the events described.

The appeal of the much-discussed Iain Hay Gordon case in 2000 is printed in *The Northern Ireland Judgments Bulletin* and available online (www.baili.org/nie/cases/NICA). This case is both comparable and connected to the Taylor case and is considered here in the Appendix.

Putting together all the material at my disposal in a readable narrative form, trying to make sense of Taylor's character and behaviour and to evoke the atmosphere of a period and a society which still live vividly in my imagination, I have occasionally veered away from a purely factual style of narration. This might irritate some purists, but not, I hope, the common reader.

To Alex and Terry, friends of my youth

To dwell on the past is to lose an eye.
To forget the past is to lose both eyes.
(Russian proverb)

Mary McGowan, 1897–1949

1

JOHN MCGOWAN HAD LAIN ill in the Royal Victoria Hospital for two weeks when on Easter Saturday, 16 April 1949, his wife Mary (aged fifty-four) was assaulted with singular brutality in their home at 18 Ponsonby Avenue, a quiet street in north Belfast. He was in the Musgrave Clinic on the following Monday when she died, the victim of what was clearly a premeditated murder. He was unable to attend either the first trial of Robert Taylor in July, when the jury of twelve men failed to return a unanimous verdict, or the retrial in October, when he was found guilty and sentenced to death. Throughout this period, Mr McGowan endured sleepless nights in hospital, assailed by images of violence. He wept silently for the obscene and wholly unexpected death of his wife, a gentle and generous woman, and reflected obsessively on how quickly everything can change in an ordered, contented life. He dreaded the void that awaited him; but for his twenty-one-year-old daughter Kathleen, an only child, he might not have retained any will to live.

During his time in hospital and nursing home, Kathleen stayed with the Caseys, family friends who lived nearby on Antrim Road. When the second trial was over and he was well enough to leave the nursing home where he had been convalescing, they returned to the house in Ponsonby. Its blood-soaked carpet had been replaced, the spattered walls scrubbed and painted. Yet the bloody past possessed it. He thought of selling it and living elsewhere, yet lacked the will to do so; he never recovered from his coronary illness and died soon after.

John McGowan was a most unusual as well as a very successful publican. He had been keen on the stage in his youth and had paid for elocution lessons when an apprentice barman; to the amusement of his wife and daughter, he would often move around the house at weekends reciting from memory long poems by Scott and Tennyson, all learned from his favourite book, *Bell's Elocution Reader*, which he kept by his bedside. But for most of those who lived in and around Ponsonby, he was a grey figure. Tied to the long hours of a pub day, he was seldom seen, and his death was hardly noticed. In the extensive newspaper reports of his wife's murder and the sensational judicial proceedings which followed, he is not mentioned by name even once: he gets a single subordinate clause which notes that 'her husband was a patient in the Musgrave Clinic at the time'. There is always more than one victim in any murder.

After his death, Kathleen sold her father's pub, The Waldorf, and the house of ill memory and left for London, never to return. She enrolled there as a student at the Royal College of Music and Drama; a love of the theatre which she inherited from her father offered an escape from bitterness and depression. The escape of her mother's killer from the legal consequences of what he had done was altogether different, being tortuous, labyrinthine, shameful and finally mysterious.

2

BETTER KNOWN IN BELFAST AS Robert the Painter, Robert Taylor was the talk of his native city from April 1949 until February 1950; and intensely so towards the end of that period. The main Northern papers – the Loyalist-Protestant trio, *The Belfast Telegraph*, *The News-Letter*, and *The Northern Whig*, and in particular the Nationalist-Catholic *Irish News* – devoted many pages to the story of this twenty-one-year-old Protestant murderer of a Catholic woman. There was interest too on the other side of the border. During the second trial and the appeal, reporters from *The Irish Press* and *The Irish Independent* in

Dublin, their editors puzzled by what they were hearing, were eventually sent north to catch up on Robert's case and take a good look at him.

Yet he managed to frustrate the camera. No clear picture of him was ever published, and those who never saw him were troubled by the missing face in the reporters' references to a 'boyish' young man (the adjective became routine), wearing always in court a white, open-necked shirt and a double-breasted blue suit. It seemed almost impossible to fit the person so described to the crime of which he stood accused. On the one occasion when a photographer, the *Belfast Telegraph's* Harry McMaster, managed to point a camera at him (as he approached the Victoria Street Register Office in February 1950), he covered most of his face with his hand. And when McMaster tried to get a close-up as he entered the building, he became violent, attacking the photographer and frustrating the attempt. His reaction prompted John Cole, the young reporter who accompanied McMaster, to exclaim to Taylor's 'best man': 'Why don't you get him inside before someone gets killed?' In a letter to his old newspaper in 2000, Cole (who covered the second trial and would later became one of the BBC's most effective political editors) wryly recalled the blundering aptness of those words.

More than Robert's face has proved elusive. Many used to speculate as to where he went after his sentence was quashed on a technicality in 1950 (Australia? England? Canada?); but then in 1969 came the Troubles, and that protracted catastrophe blasted his story and the ensuing rumours out of almost everyone's mind, an ill wind that did him much good. However, there are some alive today, of his own age or a little younger, who have reason never to forget him, and whose recollections have proved suggestive. They wonder what kind of a life he has led since his disappearance: has he enjoyed it; has he had any peace of mind? They wonder too if he is dead or alive, and if so where he lives; his history after 1950 has been a marvel of secrecy.

But there are more intriguing questions than these. Given his essential ordinariness, how does one account for the savagery of what he did on that Easter Saturday morning, at a time when murder was not commonplace in Northern Ireland? What forces within, and what forces without, made his crime possible? And what forces without facilitated his escape from the hangman's noose into safe anonymity? Is his case symptomatic of the ills which begot the Troubles? These are the kind of questions which loyal and respectable Ulster people then and now have never wanted to hear, let alone answer.

To return, however, to the missing face framed by a white open-necked shirt, and what, if anything, it might tell us if recovered. The photographic archives of the Belfast newspapers have yielded no clear picture of the young man, but the memory of a retired school teacher has helped. In the 1940s, Patrick Cassidy lived in Ponsonby Avenue and observed Taylor quite often (they were the same age and on nodding acquaintance). He offers us a surprising photofit. To Patrick and (he says) to some young Catholic girls in Ponsonby who admired the Protestant youth at a distance, his face, although somewhat thinner, seemed strikingly like that of a well-known Hollywood actor – Bobby Breen, RKO's male rival to MGM's beguiling Shirley Temple. With his mass of wavy hair and his happy smile, Bobby was the quintessence of carefree youth verging on manhood, the leading actor in half a dozen innocent movies made between 1936 and 1942 and still doing the rounds of Belfast suburban cinemas such as The Duncairn and The Lyceum in the later 1940s. His face is now available to us all thanks to the World Wide Web. Place a slender, dark-haired version of Bobby Breen's face above Taylor's blue suit and white shirt, the collar folded neatly out over the jacket in the manner thought pleasingly casual in those days (Fred Astaire as well as Bobby Breen liked it), and what we have then is a carefully composed image which both perplexes and explains.

3

TO ARRIVE AT SOME UNDERSTANDING of Taylor's crime and the strange circumstances which gave him his freedom one must look at his social background and recall the climate of political and sectarian feeling in the months prior to Easter 1949, when the murder took place.

He lived uncomfortably with his parents, his two teenage sisters, his sister's husband and their infant in a two-up, two-down in Meadow Street on the edge of the district popularly known as Tiger's Bay in North Belfast. Also in Tiger's Bay, in Lilliput Street, lived his girlfriend Lily (Elizabeth) Jones. Meadow Street was ill named, but Tiger's Bay was not; it was (and remains) an aggressively Loyalist and hotly anti-Catholic ghetto where those who faithfully returned a member of the Unionist Ascendancy at every election seldom saw the lush meadowlands where most of their political masters resided. Tiger's Bay is bounded by York Street at the city or southern end, by Halliday's Road at the top, and by Duncairn Gardens and Limestone Road on the western and eastern sides. Immediately to the north of Halliday's Road and Tiger's Bay is a group of streets usually referred to as Newington, a largely Catholic, but (at that time) peacefully mixed lower-middle-class district, bounded by Antrim Road at the top and by Duncairn Gardens and Limestone Road to the west and east. Newington comprised Newington Avenue, Newington Street, Ponsonby Avenue, Atlantic Avenue, Baltic Avenue and Lothair Avenue; to this might be added the adjacent top terrace of Duncairn Gardens, where John McGowan's friend Ned Gibbons lived. The Catholic families in Newington were bigger than the Bay families, few of which were as large as Taylor's, but their terrace houses were bigger too, and some of them had spacious rear gardens. Moreover, they were situated on an incline above the Protestant area. From the back room on the third storey of the houses on the leafy terrace on Duncairn Gardens, one could look down on the treeless streets of Tiger's Bay and see beyond them at a distance of two or three miles the shores of Belfast Lough, the skyline disfigured by black gantries. There was a wall too at the back of the houses on Newington Avenue onto which Newington children would climb and stare provokingly down into a world that none of them would dare to enter:

'Fenian rabbits, fuck off!'

'Sticks and stones
Will break my bones,
But names will never hurt me!'

'Clever shits! Fuck the pope!'

From the Tigers' point of view, this topographical arrangement must have seemed all wrong: the Taigs, the underdogs, were up there and better off. The Taig fathers in Newington included teachers, small-business men, journalists, clerks, a struggling solicitor. Thanks to the new Education Act inspired by the British Labour Party, their numerous offspring would go to grammar school and university, become very articulate, and complain more than ever about the injustices of their lot.

So when the Twelfth of July came round, the Orange march from the Lodge in Tiger's Bay through and around Ponsonby, Newington and Atlantic avenues (going nowhere but back to the Lodge) was an emotional as well as a political necessity. The Protestant men and youths marched with defiant confidence stamped on their faces, accompanied by four members of the RUC ('to preserve law and order'), two in front and two behind.

The Catholic residents and their children kept indoors, while the thunder of the Lambeg drums rattled the windows through which they stared. Unfailingly, the marchers in the late 1940s sang with special zest the old ballad of 'Dolly's Brae', a tale of fearless Orangemen, God's chosen people, who in 1849 asserted their right to march across a Catholic townland in County Down: no mere ballad, but a myth which has contributed to the shaping of Ulster's dour history since 1920:

> Lord Roden was Grand Master of the Orangemen just then,
> No better chieftain could be found among the sons of men:
> To humanists he would not yield, nor any Popish foe,
> He firmly stood like Joshua on the plains of Jericho.

> The sun did shine with splendour in a bright and cloudless
>   sky,
> Our drums did beat and fifes did play and Orange flags did
>   fly,
> Each loyal son, with sword and gun, was ready for the fray,
> When the rebel hordes attacked us going over Dolly's Brae.

In the summer of 1944, when he had turned sixteen, Robert Taylor joined his bowler-hatted and be-sashed father and uncles in the march around Newington. But he was apprenticed soon after that to Mr Barrett, a local painter and decorator, and in September was sent to Ponsonby Avenue on a job with old Jack Patterson. Between 1944 and 1948 Robert worked at many houses in north Belfast. Seven or eight of these jobs were in Ponsonby Avenue, the name with which he was to become associated. The men in the avenue with the big families did their own painting and decorating; his jobs were for the retired teacher Miss Brennan, for the widowed Mrs Shiels, Mrs Campbell, old Mr Skillen and the McGowans. The people he knew best on Ponsonby were undoubtedly the McGowans, or rather Mary McGowan and her daughter; since John McGowan would

leave for his pub at eight o'clock in the morning and would not
return until after closing-time, Robert hardly ever saw him. Like
his friends Sam Casey and Ned Gibbons, John McGowan was
one of many Catholics who had 'come up from the country' to
Belfast as young men, got themselves a job as a barman, worked
their way up to the level of manager, saved and scrimped and
bought their own pubs or off-licenses, a small one first and then
a bigger one. He worked far too hard, his wife said, so she managed all their dealings with maintenance men. As Barrett's neat
records would show, Robert worked for her in September 1944,
June 1946, May 1947 and May 1948.

At first Robert was confined to exterior jobs, sanding
woodwork and railings. And in this way he became well-known
to the locals, especially the young girls, who laughed with
pleasure when the good-looking lad gave them flirtatious winks.
With some misgivings on the part of his boss, he was allowed in
time to help Jack or one of the other time-served men with pa-
pering and painting inside. He had never been in a house like
McGowan's before he was sixteen. Nothing grand about it, but
very comfortable, plenty of room for a family of more than
three, a neat garden at the back, a cleaner who came regularly,
carpets everywhere, a piano for Kathleen, a telephone, orna-
ments, nothing wanting, the feel of money. Hardly surprising, he
would have thought: The Waldorf was a popular pub just off the
town centre, famous for its Oyster Bar.

Mary McGowan was a woman of more than usual Catholic
piety; her house was adorned with religious statues, votive lamps
and saintly pictures that spoke to Robert of the Romish idolatry
his culture despised. But he could see that everyone thought Mrs
McGowan was a decent woman, always helping and chatting. She
was generous with the biscuits at break-time, telling him he could
do with a bit of feeding; and she doted not only on Kathleen but
also on Mrs Rafferty's two little boys next door, Brendan and

John. But he found her fussy: 'You've left paint spots on the window, Robert, be sure to get them off before you go.' 'The piano's not properly covered, Robert.' And so on. These sign of disapproval rankled, and in his statement to the police he would actually complain about her complaints, as if that would somehow put him above suspicion and make him deserving of sympathy.

Barrett too started making appearances and checking up on his behaviour with other customers as well as Mrs McGowan. Warning signs of his criminal potential were obviously accumulating. His apprenticeship was for five years, but he suspected he might have to leave and find another employer before he was pushed.

As a boy Robert had been awarded prizes for good attendance at Sinclair's Seamen's Church near York Street. This was a misleading sign of persistence and reliability, due only to the fact that he was dragged there by his parents. 'Shifty' and 'slippery' were the terms which teachers and employers were apt to apply to him. He was glad to be able to leave school (Fane Street Elementary) when he was thirteen, having played truant on and off for several months before that. His first job was as a messenger boy with a leather merchant in North Street. For reasons unknown, he left that job after only one month in May 1942. His next job was as a labourer with a mineral water company, but he left that of his own accord, again after only one month. He then secured a plumber's apprenticeship and had hopes of a solid future with Sam Caughey, whose premises were conveniently located on the Antrim Road, near to his own home. This too he left of his own accord. More ominous was the way in which he parted company with his next two employers. In October 1942, after one month at Hamilton's nursery on Malone Road, he left on suspicion of thieving and in April 1944, after a year with a linen company, he was sacked on strong suspicion of having stolen from the company wages. Not having been taken to court and acquiring a criminal record by now was part of the good luck with which he seemed to be blessed.

Luck was with him too when he secured his apprenticeship at Barretts of Sunnyside Street, just off the Limestone Road. In time, however, as he would tell his pals, the shine began to wear off this job. The regular nagging from Old Jack and pernickety women about clearing this and cleaning that got on his nerves. He was sick to the teeth of Old Jack's favourite phrase, 'doin' a professional job'. But worst of all was the money. His favourite pub was The Deer's Head, which happened to be managed by John McGowan's friend, Ned Gibbons; here he could be heard complaining to his pals that he would have been almost as well off living on unemployment benefit as working. A pound a week to start with, one extra every year until you reached the basic wage of a time-served painter and decorator, a fiver a week. Once a currier in a leather factory and now a mere labourer in the shipyards, his father kept asking him for a weekly contribution, which he sometimes gave and mostly did not. Clothes, shoes, shoe repairs, a pack or two of Woodbine, a night at The Duncairn cinema with Lily: there was never enough. And French letters, which he discovered in time, were expensive. Not that they got much satisfaction there. Neither house was ever empty and Lily, he confided to his friends, didn't like climbing into Alexandra Park at night. Garrulous and boastful, he was unguarded in his talk in the pub and better known to its staff than any other of its young customers; in time he would be more talked about there than any of its clients had ever been.

4

LIFE SEEMED TO PICK UP FOR Robert when he started going with a few friends to the greyhound races at Dunmore Park. Ownership of a thoroughbred greyhound was a mark of prestige among the working class in those days. Half a dozen homes or so in Tiger's Bay had one, but competitive success was rare. Although their owners fussed about their diet and their exercise, and looked deadly serious when they marched them up Cavehill Road on Sunday mornings, these dogs were essentially pets, pretend trophies, wistful reminders of the fame and fortune brought to their owners by the likes of Ireland's great Master McGrath. But the dogs at the Dunmore meetings were the real McCoy, and with eight to ten races, one every fifteen minutes, a night there for one shilling seemed to Robert to be worth every penny. He would say that when the lure whizzed past and the dogs shot out of their traps in pursuit and the shouting became a roar, he forgot everything, his old man, the house, work, Lily, sex. For half the race the hounds were really and truly in the air, flying, just flying, with their legs crossed under them in a perfect X, their necks stretched out like the swans taking off from the lake in Alexandra Park. He shared all their excited desperation, the straining hope that showed in their noses and in every muscle and sinew of their bodies. But he said he was 'sorry too for the poor buggers, for they were fooled from the start'; they would never catch the stupid lure, they would get nothing; they were not running for themselves but for the boss-man or boss-woman who owned them. So unless you had backed the winner, the end of a race left you a bit empty, impatient for the next one. It was like sex on wet grass.

In time he realised that backing at least one winner was the only way to go home satisfied. And in this way he set foot on the path which led through betting losses and consequent theft to cold-blooded murder. Ironically, too, his fatal addiction was fed by *The Irish News.* Fervently Catholic and stridently anti-partitionist, *The Irish News* was understandably anathema in Robert's world. But its coverage of horse and greyhound racing was extremely generous (in this respect, there was nothing com-

parable to it in the Loyalist dailies) and 'Parkite', its greyhound
specialist, was probably the best tipster for dog racing in the
whole of Ireland. Thus Robert became a daily subscriber to the
Nationalist paper, furtively collecting his ordered copy every
day from The Daisy, a newsagent's shop located on York Street,
near to his home.

Although he was an impressively successful tipster, Parkite
of course didn't get it right all the time; and as Robert explained
to Billie Booth, his chief betting companion, you had to use
your own judgement in choosing if Parkite gave more than one
tip for a meeting. But for a while he won more than he lost, and
with his wage now up to three pounds in 1948, and supple-
mented by carefully distributed pilferings, he would lay one and
sometimes two bets of between one and three pounds. Some
weeks his winnings made him rich by working-class standards
and he began, it was noticed, to throw money around and talk
big. According to the police profile buried in the voluminous
material on his case in the Northern Ireland Records Office, his
big talk culminated in the extraordinary claim, swallowed by
poor Lily, if by no one else, that he had come into a legacy of
£6,000 – a sum which would have bought a mansion in those
days. He felt impatient about completing his apprenticeship and
began to talk about branching out on his own in the painting and
decorating business, buying an old van and getting married ('a
decent bed and all that').

He preferred to lay his bets at the local bookie's rather than
at the ground itself, where the odds were likely to be changed to
your disadvantage. McKee's betting office was a shack up an
alley beside the Star of the Sea convent school, on the Antrim
Road side of Halliday's Road. As Patrick Cassidy recalls,
Robert could sometimes be seen stopping on the street to light a
Woodbine and then looking around before going up the entry,
fearful perhaps of being seen by his father's friends. He must

have felt easier when he changed to Murry's, the bookmaker on Gresham Street in the town centre, not far from The Deer's Head. There was always good craic in that pub and someone to talk to about the dogs. It was there that he had chummed up again with Billie Booth, with whom he had become acquainted during his brief period at Fane Street PES on the other side of town and who, because of this relationship, would be thrust for a short while, and with considerable discomfort, on to the public stage. A lot of the talk in The Deer's Head was about the races at Celtic Park, which Robert and his friends felt was Parkite's favourite track too, perhaps because that was where greyhound racing started in Ireland back in 1927. But the Dunmore stadium was handy, just behind Alexandra Park, hardly fifteen minutes' walk from Meadow Street, whereas Celtic Park was two tram rides to the west of the city. Nevertheless, the thought of a second venue each week was tempting.

But then came that historic soccer match at Windsor Park between Belfast Celtic and Linfield – Taigs versus Prods – on Boxing Day, 1948. Nowadays, sectarian hatred in Belfast finds a unique outlet in the vicarious identification of Catholic and Protestant football fans with the fortunes of Glasgow Celtic and Glasgow Rangers respectively; weirdly, each Belfast tribal enclave has its own Celtic or Rangers supporters' club, and street violence regularly breaks out in the city when the two Scottish giants clash on the other side of the Irish Sea. This particular identification of football rivalry with sectarian and political antagonism is intimately connected with what happened at Windsor Park on 26 December 1948; it fills a void which was left by the consequences of that disastrous event.

Windsor Park, Linfield's home ground, lies only a short distance from Celtic Park, the home ground of Belfast Celtic as well as the location of the famous racing track; but the name of each park clearly announces a political allegiance and underlines the antagonism which governed relations between the supporters of both teams. Trouble began in the Boxing Day match when Celtic's big international centre forward, Jimmy Jones, crashed into Bryson, the Linfield centre half, and Bryson was carried off. There was more rough play, Celtic was awarded a disputed penalty and the game ended in a draw which the Linfield supporters thought Celtic did not deserve. Furious at the result, twenty or thirty of them climbed up the parapet on to the field before most of the players got off the pitch, then there were hundreds of them, like a great swarm of ants.

The Celtic players raced for the tunnel but were quickly surrounded; their vivid green-and-white striped jersies made them conspicuous targets. Aherne, Denvir, Lawlor and McAlinden (the goalkeeper) were badly beaten up; but the chief target and victim was Jones. He was thrown down from the parapet and might have been kicked to death if McCann, another team member, had not thrown himself on top of him and an RUC man got them through the crowd by wielding his baton. According to the newspapers next day, Ireland's great centre forward would never play again in top-class football: there would be no more internationals and no big transfer to Manchester United for him. He was cut and bruised all over and one of his legs was broken in several places; when a year later he tried to make a comeback in another Ulster team, one of his legs was noticeably shorter than the other.

Jones was the chief target of the Linfield supporters not just because he had been responsible for Bryson's departure from the field but also and mainly because he was seen as a traitor. Everyone knew that Harry Midgley, MP, the chairman of Linfield, and Joe Mackey, the club secretary, had time and again made him a generous offer and said he should be playing with his own kind and not over the road with the Taigs. But he refused to move, saying that Denvir and Lawlor were friends of his ever since he was a lad and that Celtic now had the best team ever in Ireland – they didn't win the Cup and the League every year for nothing. That did not go down well and everybody got to know about it. That he should be the player who felled Bryson on Boxing Day and denied Linfield the win they deserved seemed to set the seal on his treachery. Seldom do disappointed football fans have so clear an object on to which to vent their fury.

The day after the match, Midgley issued a statement saying that the Linfield board were disgusted by the way their fans had behaved. This response provoked much wry comment. Midgley had been a Labour MP, but he was always a passionate Orangeman and had joined the Unionists a few years before this. Indeed he had been suspended from Stormont for having a go with his fists at Jack Beattie, MP, because of the latter's Republican tirades. Midgley was known for his loathing of Catholics and Nationalists, and (at this time) for his bitter opposition to Colonel Hall-Thompson, the liberal Unionist Education Minister who favoured giving more money to the Catholic schools. It was hard to think of him as being disgusted by his supporters' response to the Celtic players, especially Jones.

Still, the Celtic board of directors did not blame Linfield for the trouble. Perhaps they were mollified by Midgley's declaration. At any rate, their response to the problem of responsibility conformed perfectly to the dynamics of Ulster's religio-political strife. Instead of the club and its supporters, they blamed the RUC, claiming that they had failed to give the Celtic players and fans enough protection; that they had hung back when the great assault began. Moreover, the board took the extraordinary and unexpected step of permanently disbanding the club, fearing an intensification of sectarian hatred and violence every time the two teams met in the future. The shock to Celtic supporters – that is, to the entirety of football-loving Catholics in the city and province – was profound.

One obvious consequence of this explosive event was that the Celtic area of Falls Road, even on a greyhound night, would not be a safe place for young Protestants: 'Hey, who are you? Are you a Catholic or a Protestant?' Robert and his friends saw that it would be the same over there as it was for Catholics in Tiger's Bay and Shankill: that question made people go white. So they confined their outings to Dunmore Park.

Robert did not stay working with Barrett, but left him in February without finishing his apprenticeship, some betting losses and related pilferings being the problem. He told Lily, his sceptical friends and his family that he was leaving because he wanted to set up on his own and be his own boss. When called to give evidence in court three months later, Barrett gave a terse account of when Robert first entered his employment, when he left and how often and with whom he worked in Ponsonby Avenue. He did not – and legally could not – say that he had sacked him because three of his customers had accused him of stealing money and that Robert, rather than have the police called in, was prudently disposed to depart without protest, leaving his boss to compensate the aggrieved customers. Already, then, a pattern was emerging, one which would not weaken his natural inclination to take risks and rely on his luck: his employers were inclined to save him from the legal consequences of his actions, thinking perhaps that it would be a pity if a nice-looking lad (and 'one of our sort') should be saddled for life with a criminal record.

But Robert was by no means grateful to Barrett. He knew all of his boss's regular customers by now and what work he had in hand for the next few months; and as some visits he subsequently made to Ponsonby Avenue suggest, he intended to do a bit of poaching in order to give himself an immediate start.

5

ONE MIGHT ASSUME THAT FROM time to time boredom and curiosity prompted Robert to investigate the rest of *The Irish News* after his daily consultation of Parkite's section on the back page. And from what he read there in the first few months of 1949 he would have found ample justification for the feelings of suspicion and hostility towards Catholics that his culture bred in him. But even if he did not stray outside Parkite's columns, he would have known from everyday talk in the city that Catholics were currently planning a political future for the province which Loyalists would have found utterly abhorrent.

Less than one week before the disastrous Celtic-Linfield match, *The Irish News* printed an item about an event in Dublin which clearly was bad news for Loyalist Ulster. The Unionist-Protestant dailies were full of it too, but *The Irish News*'s slant on the subject would have caught like barbed wire at the likes of Robert. The way this paper wrote about the new development in the ensuing weeks and months was as if Celtic were saying they were going to hammer Linfield six-nil, or that the referee should award them penalties for harmless tackles. In fact Robert might have thought that the people who wrote the paper were hoping for a really big revenge after the annihilation of their beloved team on Boxing Day. At any rate, the exceptionally bad feeling generated by the football match and its aftermath fed into and was subsumed by the overtly political conflict which unfolded over the next few months.

Looking today into *The Irish News* of that time one can see that Nationalists were suddenly energised and noisily demanding in a way they had not been since the foundation of the Unionist state in 1920, when they were condemned to – or, as Unionists would say, chose – the role of an alienated and powerless minority. The new government in Éire under John Costello was a coalition of disparate parties united by their antipathy to

Eamon de Valera, the self-conscious custodian of all things Irish. On 21 December 1948, this government set out to prove it was every bit as patriotic as Dev's party, Fianna Fáil; it did so by repealing the External Relations Act, providing thus for an eventual declaration of an Irish Republic. But this did not mean simply withdrawal from the Commonwealth, which in Unionist eyes merely set the seal on the southerners' prior withdrawal from the Union and their disloyalty to Britain, whose war against Hitler they had refused to support. No, Costello's government and legislation meant a republic of all Ireland, a republic whose constitution would clearly spell out that it was to be a Roman Catholic republic too.

And the claim to be a republic of all Ireland, with a call for the immediate unification of the country, began to be trumpeted throughout Britain, America and Europe. Practical steps were taken to effect this miracle by re-invigorating the Anti-Partition League, formed in 1945. De Valera and his party buried for the time being their resentment at losing power and joined with the new government so as to turn the League into an all-party movement.

On 27 January 1949 an all-party conference to discuss the Anti-Partition project was held at the Mansion House in Dublin, opened by the Lord Mayor, chaired by Costello and attended by eleven other leading politicians, including de Valera, General Mulcahy and the eloquent son of the legendary Maud Gonne, Sean MacBride. 'The holding of this conference is of enormous significance,' said MacBride, 'it is the first real sign of unity in the national scene since 1921' – a statement which *The Irish News* printed in bold on its front page. The paper gave full coverage to the meeting, with headline attention to the plan to set up a National Fund by subscription to aid anti-partitionist politicians in the North; the money was to be collected on the following Sunday outside all Catholic churches in the country. But most of the report was devoted to a lengthy proclamation issued at the end of the Mansion House meeting condemning in the strongest possible terms the iniquities of partition and gerrymandering.

Unlike *The Irish News*, the Unionist *Belfast Telegraph* ignored this grand document but printed what the other paper denied its readers: a large oblong picture of the twelve, dark-suited, heavy-jowled politicians at their conference table, gazing morosely at the camera. The picture seems to have been chosen because the group looked less like the Twelve Apostles than a convention of Sicilian godfathers. It was captioned, 'A Gathering in Full Strength of the Meddlers' and the names of all the criminals were printed below.

The meddlers immediately carried their campaign to England and Scotland, where exiled Irishmen organised marches and meetings in the major cities, with speeches by leading politicians from Éire and the North in which the injustices of gerrymandering and a discriminatory franchise system were heavily emphasised. As the Unionist government was quick to realise, the meddlers had started their campaign at what was a singularly propitious moment for them. A Labour government was in power in Britain. It had a much deeper distaste for the Unionist Party than it had for the English Conservatives, it was already offloading the British Empire and it might well be tempted to force the Six Counties into a marriage with the rest of Ireland. Understandably, Ulster Unionists were deeply distrustful of Clement Attlee's government and scarcely thought of it as British at all.

In some panic, Ulster's Prime Minister, Sir Basil Brooke, decided to call an early election, scheduled for 10 February 1949, its essential purpose being to function as a plebiscite which would 'show Britain and indeed the world' (he said) that the people of Ulster were thoroughly British and overwhelm-

ingly in favour of the status quo. That such an election begged
the question as to whether its inevitable outcome – a two-thirds
majority for the Unionists – was the result of a democratic procedure did not seem to trouble Sir Basil. He hurried to London
on 18 January to inform the British Prime Minister of his government's intentions and to let him know that the result of the
election should be followed by a guarantee from Westminster
that partition would not be ended without the consent of the majority of the people in the Six Counties.

6

THE ELECTION TURNED OUT TO be the province's most bit-
terly fought ever. Given that its outcome was accepted on
both sides to be inevitable, the intensity of commitment to the
charade now seems strange. But what the politicians were really
engaged in was a rhetorical contest to which it was assumed the
ears of Britain, America, Europe and even 'the world' were all
attuned. And since rhetoric was essentially more important than
electoral outcome, theatricality, hyperbole and simplification
prevailed and passions were inflamed to an extreme degree.

As reported in *The Irish News*, the anti-partitionists did
everything possible to generate fear in the Unionist camp. Their
weapon was to cry injustice and to suggest that the British Labour Party and the democratic world would no longer tolerate the
status quo in Ireland; the day of reckoning was near. The paper
explained that when Sir Basil arrived at 10 Downing Street,
Attlee was already pondering a letter from Mr A. Mulvey, the
Nationalist member for Tyrone and Fermanagh. The letter urged
that when discussing Northern Irish matters with his visitor he
should be mindful that the British Labour Party had on two occasions asserted the right to self-determination on the question of
Irish National Government; that because of a Tory-Liberal com-

bination one-fifth of the population of Ireland had frustrated the will of the other four-fifths. The paper reported too that on the same day in Stormont, the Nationalist leader James McSparran assured the Unionists that 'the tide was flowing against' them. When Harry Diamond spoke there of persecution and discrimination against the nationally minded minority, members on the government side cried 'Nonsense!'; to which he retorted that because of the present Labour Government and a great shift in British opinion, a perfect solution to the Irish question was now being sought. 'And whether the members on the opposite side want it,' he added goadingly, 'is not for them to decide. There is one thing certain: the will of the Irish people, which has been repeatedly given in the past, for the establishment of an all-Ireland republic, will eventually be carried out.'

No one at the time could miss the fact that unity and democracy were currently the most conspicuous themes in Western political discourse. On 25 January, for example, *The Irish News* reported a speech by Ernest Bevin, the British Foreign Secretary, advocating a united states of Europe, 'a new form of Western unity'; and on 29 January another speech by Paul Hoffman, US administrator for Marshall Aid in Europe, calling for 'a united Europe as the only bulwark against the totalitarian aggressor' who was now destroying the last vestiges of democracy in the countries behind the Iron Curtain. Discussions too on the formation of a larger unity still, the North Atlantic Treaty Organisation (uniting America and Canada with Western Europe) had already begun; these discussions were regularly mentioned by *The Irish News*, in part because Éire was huffily refusing to join and eager to explain why. In this year too the show-trial and conviction of Cardinal Mindszenty in Hungary, symptomatic of the general attack on Christianity in the Iron Curtain countries, seemed to focus attention sharply on the need for unity in the defence of democracy and freedom.

All this – the flowing tide – was opportune for the anti-partitionists and fed into their daily rhetoric to the chagrin of the Unionists. It prompted them to equate Sir Basil and his ministers with communist dictators and show-trial fixers, to define partition as an Iron Curtain and to claim that the Irish problem was one which the whole of the Western world would naturally want to rectify, as a kind of logical first step to a better world. *The Irish News* reported de Valera's 'fine speeches' in Birmingham in which he asked the English 'to turn their eyes to the problem of democracy in Ireland rather than Eastern Europe.' 'Britain and Ireland,' he said, 'can cooperate in the service of Western Union when, and only when, the question of domination and partition is resolved.'

7

ON 24 JANUARY *THE IRISH NEWS* was pleased to report on its front page that Norman Porter, organiser of the fundamentalist National Union of Protestants, had decided to contest the Clifton seat in North Belfast (adjacent to the Duncairn Ward in which Tiger's Bay was located); he was challenging the Official Unionist candidate and sitting MP, Colonel Hall-Thompson, the Minister whose education proposals were seen by the Orange Order as being intolerably generous to Catholics. 'Notwithstanding Sir Basil Brooke's appeal for unity amongst Unionists, it is evident that the rank and file are far from being united,' crowed the paper.

Unity on the Protestant side was to become an obsession with Sir Basil's government. It wanted to show Westminster and the world a one-hundred-percent endorsement from 'the people of Ulster' (his term for its Protestant population) of its partitionist stance. The threat to Loyalist unity came not only from religious extremists like Porter and a few other Independent Unionists but also from the Northern Ireland Labour Party and the Protestant working class. When Robert's father was passing Sam Mawhinney's house on Upper Meadow Street, he would stop, rattle his larynx and spit ostentatiously on the ground. For Mawhinney was a Protestant who never joined the Order and had now been reported in *The Belfast Telegraph* as seconding the candidacy of a Labour man, Hugh Downey, a Catholic who was running against a Unionist in Dock Ward. To keep the working class on its side was not as easy for the ultra-conservative Unionist Party as it had been hitherto, now that Ulster was experiencing the social benefits of a Labour government – completely free medicine, hospitalisation, glasses and dental treatment.

The party's rhetorical strategy was to spread fear among Protestants and invoke the image of a siege in which petty differences are put aside and every man, woman and child rallies to defend the community against fifth columnists and an external enemy. 'This is no ordinary election,' declared Lord Glentoran, chairman of the party, to his constituents in Bloomfield, 'our very existence depends on it' (reported *The Belfast Telegraph*). Speaking in support of Glentoran, Brian Faulkner, a future Prime Minister, invoked the great myth which has always embodied this Loyalist theme. To cheers from the crowd, he declared: 'We will give them' – Costello and his interfering henchmen – 'the answer of the thirteen Apprentice Boys [at the siege of Derry in 1689]: "No surrender".' This was no time for fuzzy liberal notions, suggested Brian Maginess, barrister, Minister of Home Affairs, Attorney General (1956–1964) and County Court Judge (1964–67); the only alternative to submission to Dublin and Rome, and all the shenanigans which that entailed, was tough, uncompromising Orangeism: 'The rattle of Orange drums is preferable to the tinkle of money on a plate outside the church door.' The so-called 'chapel-gate' collection in aid of the anti-partition candidates was seized on generally by Unionist orators as proof that a united Ireland meant domination by Rome: 'Home Rule, Rome Rule', as the old saying went.

On 1 February, Sir Basil praised the unselfishness of those Independent Unionists who were stepping down in order to close ranks against the common enemy. He mentioned no names but was clearly referring at that moment to the dangerous Norman Porter, who was bent on toppling the 'liberal' Minister of Education. Porter withdrew his candidacy for Clifton with a great show of loyalty, although he was merely bottling his sectarian feelings for the time being. Shortly after the election he would be instrumental in forcing Hall-Thompson's resignation as Minister of Education and installing the pugnacious Linfield chairman, Harry Midgley, in his place. He would also contest and win Hall-Thompson's seat for himself, standing as an Independent Unionist.

Another danger which the government had in mind was absenteeism, whether due to complacency ('We always win') or disillusion ('A plague on both your houses!'). Hall-Thompson addressed this problem in the standard party manner when he told his constituents in North Belfast that to abstain or to vote against an Official Unionist candidate would be counted in Westminister and Éire as indicating a willingness to join the Irish Republic: 'Beware the precipice!' Contained in this warning, however, was an implicit allusion to his Protestant Labour opponent in Clifton ward, who, like other Labour candidates, was harping on the subject of unemployment and the ills of a stagnant economy. Unionist Headquarters in Glengall Street sought to neutralise criticism of the party's social and economic record with a leaflet entitled 'A Warning to the Ulster People' in which it emphasised (correctly) the inferiority of social services in Éire to those in the North; copies were dispatched by train, bus and lorry to all corners of the province. Naturally, no credit was given to the Labour Party for its welfare legislation – neither in this leaflet, nor in the rally speeches of Sir Basil when he emerged from his thousand-acre estate to assure voters that 'the Unionist government has worked untiringly for the good of *all* the people of Ulster'.

The Protestant working class, however, was moved less by socio-economic claims than by the rhetoric of cultural annihilation, with its militaristic myths of embattlement, singlemindedness and victory. So Sir Basil, sometime captain in the British army, urged them to 'cross the Boyne with me as your leader and fight the same cause as King William fought in days gone by'. And he flattered and cajoled his footsoldiers: 'Campaigns are planned by military commanders and their staffs, but the fighting is done by the rank and file.' The Minister of Education literalised Sir Basil's historical-military metaphor by riding up Duncairn Gardens and Cliftonville Road on a white horse, projecting himself to his constituents as a spiritual descendant of the great Orange King. (In *The Irish News* of 16 April, the waggish 'Professor Stormont' continued his satiric history of Ulster with an Orangeman's view of '1690 and All That', noting that 'Near Drogheda William borrowed a white horse from his aide, Colonel Hall-Thompson.')

Inevitably the militarist rhetoric begot violence: sticks and stones that break bones. Most but not all of the violence was directed against anti-partition candidates and their supporters. On 8 February, Jack Beattie, the Linfield chairman's punchbag at Stormont, was a victim of physical as well as verbal abuse once more. Campaigning near the city centre, he was hit by a stone and missed by a log; he donned an engineer's helmet and stubbornly continued speaking for a time while a section of the crowd sang a familiar Orange ballad, 'The Sash My Father Wore', but he eventually retreated. Other meetings were similarly disrupted and disbanded. James McSparran, chairman of the Anti-Partitionist League, accused the opposition in the League's manifesto of 'a planned campaign of violence, tumult and intimidation to break up meetings and destroy free speech'. *The Irish News* gave full coverage to the subject and so did Éire's *Irish Press* and *Irish Independent*, but *The Belfast Telegraph* responded: 'Nationalists Sink to New Depths in Smear Campaign'. It quoted the Unionist Chief Whip, Mr W.B. Topping, KC, who described the manifesto as 'a despicable document which should reveal to the world the minds of those who are trying to enslave the free people of Ulster'; Sir Basil simultaneously claimed that 'the language used by the Nationalists and their press in attempting to discredit Northern Ireland and its people has revolted many electors' (*Belfast Telegraph*, 9 February 1949).

When all the votes were counted after the election, it was clear that the Labour candidates' insistence on the failure of the government to deal with the problems of unemployment and housing had meant nothing to a Protestant working class terrified by the thought of subjugation in an economically inferior, priest-ridden state. Nor was absenteeism among the rest of the Protestant electorate a problem. The poll was the highest ever in the history of the state, and the government was returned with a three-to-one majority (thirty-two seats as against eleven for the anti-partitionists), with increased majorities in all the wards contested and with fourteen Unionist candidates returned unopposed. In Duncairn Ward (which embraces Tiger's Bay), Grant's majority over his Labour opponent was increased seven-fold, Hall-Thompson's in nearby Clifton was doubled. The Party's debt to all Loyalists, but especially to the working class, was immense.

'The greatest electoral triumph in our history,' said Sir Basil. 'We have just emerged from a battle in which Ulster has declared to the whole world, "I am master of my fate. I am captain of my soul".' The Nationalists comforted themselves with the bitter knowledge that they had foreseen the worst (hardly consistent with their assertion that partition's days were numbered) and by claiming the moral high ground, hammering more insistently than ever on the wickedness of gerrymandering and the denial of one-man, one-vote. The Dublin government responded by condemning the election as a fraud and announcing that Ireland would be officially proclaimed a Republic on Easter Monday, 18 April. That date was the thirty-third anniversary of the Easter 1916 Rising. It was also the day on which, for entirely unpolitical reasons, Robert Taylor would choose to get married and on which he would, instead, be charged with the murder of a Catholic woman.

For the Unionists, gerrymandering and a discriminatory franchise system were simple necessities, instruments without which their control of the scissored six counties would be seriously endangered; so they did not allow any scruples or accusations on such matters to affect their triumphant mood. Nor did the Labour government take them to task on these matters. Rather, it gave them what they wanted: an act of parliament promising that Northern Ireland would not cease to be part of the United Kingdom without the consent of its own parliament.

8

DELIVERING LEAFLETS, HECKLING speakers and lighting bonfires, Sir Basil's humble footsoldier, Robert Taylor, was caught up in the passions of the contest and the euphoria of victory. But for the time being he enjoyed none of the fruits of this great electoral triumph. Payback time (if such it was and not just good luck) would come later. Sacked by Barrett a few days after the election, he was no better off now than the unemployed Catholics who constantly presented themselves as the victims of Protestant discrimination at the workplace. And, like his father, he firmly believed that these disloyal moaners and their friends in the IRA were somehow responsible for the difficulties of the Protestant working class. They felt it was thoroughly unjust if a Catholic, who was by definition opposed to the state, had a job while a single Protestant was unemployed. ('All Catholics are traitors,' said Midgley, the Education Minister-in-waiting),

The shock of losing his job with Barrett was followed by another of far greater magnitude, and one which made money and employment a matter of extreme urgency. He had taken one risk too many in the dark in Alexandra Park. Lily was pregnant and terrified. Her family was furious and made it clear that they did not want the disgrace of an illegitimate birth and the burden of an abandoned daughter and grandchild on their hands. Those old enough to recall the 1940s and 1950s know that the stigma of illegitimacy and the associated misery of the unmarried mother constituted then one of the most inhuman features of Christian Ireland and Britain.

The marriage had to take place as soon as possible and they had to find somewhere to live. Robert's sister Madeline and her husband, James Connor, were moving out of Meadow Street on Easter Saturday into a house they had secured on nearby Mervue Street and were willing to rent him and Lily a room until they could afford a place of their own. So the wedding day was fixed for Easter Monday, 18 April. A church wedding was decided on, perhaps because a registry office would mean going into town and would cost more in taxis; or perhaps in order to appease the parents with a gloss of respectability. Lily had never been a church goer, but the minister at St Barnabas' Church on lower Duncairn Gardens, impressed by Robert's prizes for attendance at Sinclair's Seamen's Church, agreed to perform the service.

Robert got some work from his mother's friend Mrs Walker of Syringa Street in Tiger's Bay; but with only two months until the wedding, he knew he had to get more lucrative employment in the better-class homes up the Cliftonville or the Antrim Road; or in Newington, whose Catholic residents, he assumed, would be in a compliant mood now that Nationalists had been been sent a stern message. Obviously he had to select someone who had not accused him of stealing, and Mrs McGowan was one such. He knew that Barrett was due to do some work for her in March or April, depending on progress with other jobs.

So on 19 February, three days before his twenty-first birthday, he knocked at her door. It was opened by Kathleen, to whom he cheerfully explained that he had come to fix a time for decorating the bedrooms and any other bits and pieces of work her mother had in mind. 'It's Robert the painter,' Kathleen called to her mother. 'Oh, has he come already?' she responded. Yes, he said, he had left Barrett and he and his brother were setting up business together. His only brother happened to be in the RAF, which he had joined in 1938, but Robert obviously thought that the family fiction would be a persuasive opener; the brother could 'fall ill' when the work began. Wiping her hands on her apron, Mary McGowan came to the door and asked him if he had finished his apprenticeship. He assured her that he had; nevertheless, she said she would have to keep to her arrangement with Mr Barrett, who had done her work for so long. She was sorry and she wished him well. The Bobby Breen smile disappeared. 'Oh, if that's the way you want it, okay,' he said. He turned quickly and banged the gate behind him, leaving mother and daughter feeling uncomfortable. Robert's sense of the right order of things was clearly outraged.

Walking into town each week via Duncairn Gardens and York Street to collect his unemployment allowance of £1.6s, Robert passed three establishments whose owners were to play important parts in his legal history. First of these was McKenzie's grocery shop (this name has been changed), located at the corner of Duncairn Gardens and Halliday's Road and patronised by the Protestants of Tiger's Bay; exactly opposite stood McHughes's grocery, patronised by Newington Catholics. As a boy, Robert would many times have watched the jovial McKenzie slicing bacon with cool efficiency on his gleaming Berkel, or shovelling sugar with a pewter scoop and casual accuracy into stiff paper bags. But he had disappointed Robert when he left school by not selecting him for the vacant job of messenger boy; in time, however (as local opinion had it), McKenzie, a juryman in his first trial, would superabundantly compensate him for this disappointment.

Next came The Daisy on York Street; its owner, Robert Clarke, another co-religionist, would have been commercially prudent enough not to tease him about his daily purchase of *The Irish News*. But when questioned by the police on Easter Saturday, and later in court, he would be very precise in giving evidence that told heavily against his young customer. Just across the road from The Daisy was Morrison's pub, a halfway house into which Robert would drop for a pint of porter and some eager scrutiny of the back page of *The Irish News*. He would favour Alexander Morrison with his opinions on this and that, and seemed to infer from the publican's willingness to listen that he had a friend to whom he might turn in time of need (which he would do). His last port of call during these days of unemployment, after collecting his money from 'the Boroo', was The Deer's Head. Here he and Billie Booth and one or two others, perched on high stools and leaning on the bar, would compare notes on current form and discuss winnings and losses before Robert's opinions, prejudices and complaints were aired.

When he was sacked by Barrett in February, Robert had £30 saved in the Post Office, but his losses at Dunmore left him with no more than five pounds as the Easter wedding approached. He had assured Lily's unemployed father that he would be able to pay for the wedding expenses himself. He had promised

Madeline and John that he could pay for the room in their place, assuring them he was bound to be getting regular work by then. And he had to buy Lily a ring. His father was unable to lend him any money and the two young sisters earned a pittance at Gallaher's tobacco factory. His brother in the RAF could probably afford to help but disapproved of him and would be certain to refuse a loan; he would in fact keep well clear of Belfast when his cocky young sibling got into serious trouble.

But Robert perforce went ahead with the wedding plan, hoping his luck would turn and that all would be well on the day. He came to an arrangement with Houston and Williamson, a firm of taxi hirers which catered (in this instance with curious aptness) for both funerals and weddings. Its office was located just above the Courthouse and the Gaol at 138 Crumlin Road. The firm has since moved further up the road and still functions, but the nearby Gaol and Courthouse are boarded up and in decay, grim relics of ancient crimes, Robert's included. His choice of that company was oddly prophetic.

Robert told John Williamson how many would be attending the wedding in a formal capacity; and as if money could never be problem, nonchalantly accepted Williamson's professional advice on what would be deemed appropriate in the circumstances: four cars, two bouquets, four ladies' sprays and three gents' buttonholes – the price, £12. He explained that he would be unable to pay in advance and persuaded Williamson to accept an arrangement whereby he would pay the £12 not later than the Saturday before the wedding. Although Williamson would say in court that £12 or £13 was not excessive expenditure for a working-class wedding, and was careful to say nothing even vaguely critical of the young man, he was privately surprised that someone who seemed a mere youth was getting married and that he, and not his prospective father-in-law, was in charge of all the financial arrangements.

Robert's continued search for work, either immediate or for the post-wedding period, was unsuccessful. His slight physique and youthful appearance were probably a disadvantage in the eyes of prospective employers, outweighing the effect of his confident manner. The Deer's Head manager was one of those who said 'sorry'; he explained that he always used McFaul's – a Falls Road firm, Catholic of course. As the long workless days went by, feelings of desperation took possession of him. In the pub, he was not the cocky, loquacious Robert of old, but noticeably irritable and withdrawn.

Holy Week arrived. On Monday, exactly one week before the appointed wedding day, he received a jolting letter from Houston and Williamson; with its quaint detail and exacting tone intact, an excerpt would be read out in court a few months later:

Dear Mr Taylor,

With respect to your arrangements for Easter Monday, 18th inst., we write to inform you that the price of carnations has risen unexpectedly since you placed your order, so that the sum now due amounts to £12. 9s. We would also like to remind you that, as agreed, this sum has to be paid before the wedding, and not later than Easter Saturday, 16th inst. We would greatly appreciate therefore if you would call in our office to complete the arrangement at your earliest convenience or <u>on that date at the latest</u>.

Yours faithfully,

John Williamson.

Just how much money he had at this point is uncertain, but from the evidence emerging in his admissions under police interrogation and during cross-examination in court, it would seem that it was not nearly enough to cover his expenses. His only hope now was in one last successful bet at the races. The advert in the *Irish News* on Thursday morning ran appealingly as usual: 'Tonight. Attractive Mid-Week Card. Comfortable Seating. Accommodation with Perfect View of Racing. Seven Races either 435 or 525 yards. First Race 7.30.' Parkite's only tip was for Mrs Framton's Derryboy Traveller in the Downview Stakes, Bought At to come second. Robert decided to rely on Parkite, the tipster more often right than wrong.

Thursday evening was beautifully mild; a warm and sunny weekend was forecast, splendid for Easter trippers and newly weds. As Robert set out hopefully in the direction of Dunmore, a cloudless sunset softened the harsh brick-red of the little streets and dazzled the windows of the poor. In Dunmore, as at all greyhound races, the banter drew everyone, owners and bookies as well as punters, into a democracy of pleasure and excitement. Robert, however, would not have joined in the banter but would have sat apart, tensely waiting for the outcome of the fourth race, an outcome on which his whole future – and a good woman's life – depended. He would have left the stadium in rage and despair before the meeting ended: Derryboy Traveller came second, Bought At first, reversing Parkite's predictions. He would assure the police that he had £5 left on Saturday morning, intimating thus that his financial situation was not completely dire on the day of the murder; but the prosecution lawyer may have been right in suggesting that he had less than £1.

On the day after the race, Good Friday, he found no way out of his predicament and did nothing. Loquacious though he was, he had told none of his drinking friends about his hasty wedding and approached none of them for a loan, perhaps knowing they would not or could not help, perhaps because asking for help was a humiliation he couldn't face after all his bragging about an inheritance, wins at Dunmore and sex in the park. On Saturday morning, however, he was decisive; the reckless, all-or-nothing mood of the gambler took over. After breakfast he walked down to Morrison's, knowing that he would find the publican alone at that hour or at least easy to draw aside for a private word. He explained that he had lost a big bet on Thursday, that he was getting married on Monday and would appreciate the loan of £20 (£12.9s for the taxi firm, £4 or £5 for a wedding ring, a few pounds for drinks). Astonished, the publican said that that was four weeks' wages for his man and as much as he could clear for himself and his family in a week; he had his own problems; he could not oblige; sorry.

Rebuffed, but hardly surprised, Robert made straight for home and prepared for what he now thought to be the only solution to his problem. From his bag of assorted tools and materials in the coal hole under the stairs he took a piece of tough cord, seven feet long, and from his brother-in-law's kitbag a heavy spanner, with its unusual marking: 'F33 seven-eighths spanner, forged in USA'. He put the cord in one pocket of his overcoat, slid the spanner into the other, then found a pair of gloves and headed up Duncairn Gardens in the direction of Ponsonby. He entered Ponsonby at the top end – the opposite end from McGowan's – by way of a zig-zag alley that connects Newington with Halliday's Road. The houses seemed asleep in the morning sunshine, the street empty save for two young girls playing ball against the gable-end of Ponsonby's topmost house, Lola Slevin and Anne Gibbons. He may have thought they failed to notice him as he made his way down the avenue on the other side. Anne was the daughter of Ned Gibbons, the Deer's Head manager; her life-long interest in Robert's story dates from this moment.

9

LIKE ROBERT, MARY MCGOWAN had spent a troubled night; and, like him, she woke to make a fateful decision, one which helped to seal their joint destiny. In court it would be revealed that she was alone in the house on the day she was assaulted, since her husband was in hospital and her daughter had gone by bus to visit her uncle, who lived alone in a remote part of the country between Newry and Crossmaglen, a distance of sixty miles or so. What was not revealed in court is that she woke Kathleen very early, telling her she feared that something unfortunate might happen or could have happened to her brother Dan, who could not be contacted quickly, not having a telephone. She wanted Kathleen to go to him right away and check whether all was well with him. Perhaps her husband's heart attack of two weeks earlier was responsible for this frame of mind. But Kathleen had long since been led to believe that her mother had some kind of sixth sense; on several occasions she had had premonitions which seemed to have been borne out by events. So she made no objection to her mother's strange request and, being of an affectionate and easy disposition, said she would be very willing to go. Her mother told her she could get the 8.00 am bus to Newry from Smithfield and be back at 4.00 pm, in time for their evening visit to the hospital. To make sure that she caught the bus, she would leave her to the station. That she should be so anxious about her brother's welfare on this of all days would always seem strange to her daughter.

When Kathleen had dressed and come downstairs, the table was set for what would be their last meal together: a breakfast of tea, boiled eggs and bread that the mother was slicing with a carving knife as she entered the kitchen. After the meal, they departed quickly, leaving the dishes and cutlery to drip-dry by the sink in the scullery. They caught a tram into town, got off at Royal Avenue and reached the Smithfield bus station with fifteen minutes to spare. Mary gave Kathleen £4.10s, a substantial sum of money (her weekly household allowance was £5), much more than was necessary to cover the return fare for the bus journey to Newry and from Newry to the farm. This was a sign of her strange anxiety; another sign was her parting gesture. As her daughter stepped on to the bus, she took her mother-of-pearl rosary beads from her bag and pressed them into her hand. Kathleen would say many prayers on those beads over the years; they included, some months later, a battery of prayers to the Mother of God that would astonish most people.

On the tram that would take her back to Ponsonby Avenue, Mary had a copy of *The Irish News*, bought at the stand in the bus station. 'Ireland a Republic on Monday', said the front page headline; great celebrations were planned all over what would soon be the former Free State. On the same page the beautiful weather was forecast to continue and twenty trains, it was said, were being laid on by the Great Northern Railway to take holiday makers to Bundoran, Dublin, Dun Laoghaire and Arklow. But she was indifferent to politics, having always voted as her husband said she should; and she would certainly have been untouched by the holiday mood. She would get back to Newington in time to attend the Easter Saturday ceremonies at the Holy Family Church, pray for her husband and brother, and replenish her store of the baptismal water blessed by the priest on that morning. In the Preface of the day's mass she would hear the priest intone:

> O God, whose spirit in the very first beginnings of the world did brood over the waters, giving the element of water, even in its origin, the power to sanctify; who by water didst wash away the crimes of a guilty world, and by the outpouring of the flood didst signify regeneration, so that the same element might

> have the mysterious power to make an end of vice and
> a beginning of virtue . . .

Unlike Kathleen, she never really enjoyed her husband's poems, but said she was always soothed and uplifted by the language of church ritual and the repetitive sequence of the rosary.

Alighting from the tram at the stop where Antrim Road and Duncairn Gardens converge, she went into the empty house to put away the breakfast dishes and collect a container for the holy water. She chose a mineral water bottle, the solid, old-fashioned type with a white ceramic top permanently affixed to the neck but easily flicked open. In the Holy Family church, seventeen-year-old Gerald Dowd from Ponsonby Avenue, an ex-altar boy, had been called back that morning to supervise his young successors in a particularly long and complicated set of ceremonies. At the end, Mary, with a smile of recognition, handed him her bottle to be filled. Last things have a way of rooting themselves in the memory: like Kathleen and the moment when her mother placed the rosary beads in her hand as she boarded the bus, Gerald would remember this moment all his life. On Monday he would be asked by Detective Head Constable Thornton if he recognised a broken bottle which the detective said was used in the assault on Mrs McGowan. Gerald recognised the white ceramic top on which was inscribed the name of Corry's Mineral Water Company.

Back in Ponsonby after the Mass of the Pre-Sanctified, Mary McGowan met her friend and next-door neighbour Mrs Rafferty and joined her for a quick cup of tea and a chat, while the four-year-old twins, John and Brendan, ran in and out from the back garden. She then returned to her own house, put some of the holy water in the little font on the wall near the front door and began preparations for an evening meal: boiled chicken, potatoes and vegetables, with chicken soup to start. She set the chicken and the carving knife on the scullery board and filled a large pot of water and barley, leaving it on a slow gas to come to the boil while she went out on two small errands. The other vegetables and the chicken would be added on her return.

The rest of her movements on that morning would become public knowledge, many times described over the following months. She crossed over Atlantic Avenue to Madden's green-grocery on 231 Antrim Road, bought some fruit and waited out-side to collect her bread from Bernard McKeever, the Kennedy's Bakery man who normally parked there for an hour at midday, eating his lunch inside his electrically driven van. Since she would be visiting her husband in the afternoon, when McKeever usually delivered the bread to her house, she had arranged to get it from him on Saturday at this stopping point. It was now almost 12.00 noon. While she was waiting for McKeever, Robert, who had seen her leaving the house, caught up with her and stopped to exchange a few civil words, showing no trace of the resent-ment he had displayed at the close of their last encounter and no doubt nurtured ever since. He would have assumed that her hus-band was at work and one might conjecture that he managed to learn from her that Kathleen was away for the day; if not, then he must have concluded ten minutes later, when he found her alone in the house, that his luck was definitely in.

Leaving her at Madden's, he walked up the Antrim Road in the opposite direction to Ponsonby. But he made a right turn into Baltic Avenue and circled back into Atlantic and towards Ponsonby. It was now approximately 12.05. At that moment, Mrs Shiels of 28 Ponsonby Avenue (for whom he had done work on two occasions) had just left the Holy Family church in Newington Avenue; she caught sight of him as he emerged from Baltic. He looked around him and then preceded her on the op-posite side of Atlantic Avenue before he crossed over and dis-appeared into Ponsonby. She noticed he was wearing distinc-tively coloured shoes – 'very light in colour, light yellow' (she would say in court) – and a belted blue overcoat, the collar turned up. By the time she herself rounded the corner into Ponsonby to go home, he was no longer visible.

Mary had hardly removed her coat and reached the kitchen when she heard a knock at the door. It was Robert. He needed to make a call urgently, he said, and asked to use her phone, probably saying he had no change for the call box on Duncairn. She agreed and as she turned towards the kitchen, leaving him to pick up the phone in the hall, he closed the door behind him, drew the cord from his pocket, put it round her neck, pulled her backwards towards him, twisted it round twice and pulled as hard as he could. He must have thought she would expire quickly (killing seems so easy on the screen), but she was able to stamp hard on his feet and put her hands over her shoulders, tearing at his face and leaving scratches on both sides. To accelerate the cord's work, he stuffed a gloved hand down her throat and tried to choke her. In the struggle, her lower dentures shot on to the floor. She pulled away from him with a strength which must have surprised him (she was no bigger than himself and not stocky, but as Kathleen agreed in court, she was vigorous and strong). He then abandoned the attempt at strangulation and followed her as she staggered into the kitchen. Here he attacked her with the spanner, which seems to have slipped from his gloved hand. She got as far as the scullery and was making for the back door when he grabbed the bottle containing holy water and crashed it over her head.

Then he saw an instrument guaranteed to kill – the carving knife. It rose and fell, rose and fell, rose and fell: on skull, face, arms, neck. But it struck hard against bone and bent, so he threw it away. At this point apparently, he began to punch her in the face, fracturing her nose and causing both eyes to bleed and close. She collapsed in a heap on the floor, all of her visible flesh now hidden by the gushing blood. He then began to kick her in the ribs, back and arms, and desisted when he noticed the pot of soup bubbling on the gas. This he took and emptied over her, leaving her with multiple burns and causing pain so extreme that she would never allude to the gaping wounds from which she bled so profusely; in their gratuitous cruelty, these last actions seem to have been fuelled by a terrible combination of frustration and hatred. He must have inferred from the choking noises she was making that she was near to death by now; but to make doubly sure, he opened the oven, turned the gas up full and closed the scullery door behind him.

In the kitchen (i.e. living room) he found her handbag. Nothing but coins. He can hardly have counted them, for as would be recorded later in a policeman's dry prose, it contained less than one pound – exactly thirteen shillings and ten pence: an infuriatingly small sum for someone who anticipated a clutch of notes – holiday-weekend money and housekeeping. He left the coins. Dashing upstairs to the bedrooms, he tore open an attaché case and then drawers, hoping to find notes, unbanked takings from the shop perhaps. Nothing. Letters and invoices. Brooches, necklaces, gold cuff links, that sort of thing ('it was the sort of house where you would expect to find valuables,' said Detective Sergeant Davis in court). These were useless in the circumstances: immediate cash was what he needed, a visit to a pawnbroker would be fatal. Then he heard movement below in the scullery, the door latch clinking. From the landing window he saw that his victim had regained her feet, had staggered out into the yard and was groping her way towards the door into the garden. Moreover, someone from next door was looking over the hedge into her garden. Returning to the front bedroom, he checked for movement in the avenue, hurried downstairs and closed the door quietly behind him. No one recalled seeing him as he headed up Ponsonby and slipped down into Tiger's Bay via the zig-zag route at the top of the avenue. The two young girls playing at the gable-end had been sent on an errand to McHugh's.

It was now 12.20. In a ten-minute storm of brutality whose origins would always seem mysterious to many, Robert Taylor had effectively ended a life, and had drastically and for ever changed his own life and the lives of some others. And got nothing. The practical reasons for the murder are obvious, but to explain the sheer savagery of the deed we must consider Robert's hatred of a nagging Catholic woman who had refused to give him work when he desperately needed it and now stubbornly refused to die quickly; and we must look beyond that to the kind of attitude expressed by a middle-aged woman as she waited outside the Courthouse for his trial in July. It is a remark rooted in the memory of Pascal O'Hare, then a young law student, who stood nearby: 'Good Fenian crop in the soil.'

10

ROBERT SKILLEN OF 16 PONSONBY Avenue, Mary McGowan's other next-door neighbour, enjoyed his retirement. Daily mass, household chores and work in the garden filled his day and helped to close out those thoughts of mortality which become invasive when the preoccupations of workaday life are removed. The first thing he did each morning was to look down with satisfaction from the rear bedroom window on the effects of yesterday's work in the garden. This Easter Saturday morning he would have found his tasks there particularly pleasant. His forsythia and his golden primulas and pansies were brilliant in the sunshine, and after a few dry days the lawn was ready for its first mowing of the year. It all fitted his mood. He had just told a young neighbour that bad memories – of the sectarian riots and assassinations in 1935 and the 1941 air raids which obliterated the houses opposite and killed many families in the vicinity – had at last given way to a sense of peace and tranquillity. And indeed Northern Ireland was entering what historians of the period now call 'The Quiet Years'.

Perhaps because of the lawn mower and his partial deafness, he seems not to have heard the first screams; when he did hear a choking cry and turned round to look, Mrs McGowan was stumbling down her garden, clearly visible over the hedge. Not that she was recognisable as Mary McGowan. When he dashed round to help her, he noticed the little Rafferty boys transfixed by what they saw and told them to fetch their mother immediately; they ran in and told her there was 'a red lady' in the garden next door; they were not thinking of the kindly woman who had sipped tea in their house a short time earlier.

When Mrs Rafferty entered her own garden, Mr Skillen was already there, supporting Mrs McGowan and moving in her direction. Together, they helped the stricken woman to a sitting position at the bottom of the three steps leading from the garden to the yard. As Mrs Rafferty would testify in court, the first thing she herself said when she found it possible to speak was: 'Who are you?' To which her neighbour replied, between choking gasps, 'Don't you know me? . . . I'm Mrs McGowan.' 'She didn't look like a human being at all,' whispered Mrs Rafferty in court, still evidently in awe of the remembered spectacle.

The head, face and clothing of the woman she supported in her arms were covered in blood mixed with barley. Blood continued to flow freely from the wounds, oozing even from her ears and her closed eyes. She tugged feebly at the doubled cord around her neck and gasped repeatedly for breath. An earring and the leg of a pair of spectacles were lodged grotesquely in her hair. Her shoes were missing.

Mrs Rafferty eased the blood-soaked cord on her neck and bathed her face lightly with water brought by Mr Skillen; but she was unable to staunch the flow of blood. Mrs McGowan asked for water to drink but vomited blood when she swallowed it. Later they helped her indoors and got her into an armchair where her head was supported by Mrs Rafferty.

'Who did this to you?'

'Robert did it.'

'Robert who?'

'Robert the painter. I don't know his second name. . . . He works for Barrett of Sunnyside Street. . . . Miss Brennan knows his other name. . . . He lives in Upper Meadow Street, I think.'

And then:

'Kathleen's in Newry. . . . I'm dying. . . . Don't let her come here. . . . Meet her at four. . . . I'm going to die. . . . Phone Mick in the shop and tell him what's happened. . . . Poor Daddy, he'll get a terrible shock . . .'

Mrs Rafferty accompanied her to the Mater Hospital in the ambulance. She assured her friend that she would get better when the doctors attended to her, but Mary McGowan said, 'No, I'm dying.' She thanked Mrs Rafferty for her kindness, mentioned her little boys concernedly and seemed to lose consciousness before being carried into the hospital.

*

When Mary McGowan was collecting her bread outside the greengrocer's, all was quiet in the police barracks which stood directly opposite on the other side of Antrim Road. Detective Sergeant Hugh Davis was in the day room chatting over a cup of tea with the station sergeant and two constables. Trouble on the streets had died down since the election and they anticipated a relatively peaceful weekend, though they wondered if the Republican celebrations down South might not spark off some trouble this side of the border on Sunday or Monday. Davis, however, was looking forward to a week's holiday on the Isle of

Man, starting on Monday. 'Hope the weather holds for you,' remarked a colleague.

At 12.30 Davis was putting on his cycle clips, preparatory to a ride round the district, when John Caughey burst in. A journalist who worked for *The Belfast Telegraph*, Caughey lived at 22 Ponsonby Avenue, next door to Mrs Rafferty. He was a small, earnest man, a deeply religious Presbyterian and a proud Loyalist, but a good friend of Mrs McGowan and Mrs Rafferty, 'nice women who never talked politics'. He was out of breath and extremely agitated. He had been in his kitchen when he heard the cries of distress in the adjacent gardens and hurried down to investigate. He too would say in court that he did not recognise the horrific figure that Mrs McGowan had become, although he had known her for twenty years. Davis returned with him to Ponsonby and they went first to the McGowan house. They noticed a set of lower dentures in the hall, a large spanner on the kitchen floor and a handbag lying open on the table. 'The scullery was a shambles,' said Caughey. There was a carving knife on the draining board, the blade bent, both handle and blade all covered in blood. On the floor were an earring in a clot of blood and a chicken ready for cooking. Broken spectacles lay beside the cooker. The oven door was open and the gas turned on but not lit. Blood covered most of the floor and was splashed over the walls as high up as the ceiling. Next door they found Mrs Rafferty sitting on the steps at the back of the garden supporting a woman covered in blood and soup, gasping for breath, her eyes blackened, swollen, closed and bleeding, with lumps of flesh gouged from the face and mouth.

Davis immediately phoned police headquarters in Glenravel Street for help and was told that District Inspector Reid and Detective Head Constable Thornton and an ambulance would be up immediately. Returning to Mrs McGowan, he noticed the blood-soaked cord hanging loose about her neck (he thought at first that it was 'some kind of religious emblem'); when some of the blood was sponged off, he concluded that she had been badly beaten as well as hacked about the face. But he inferred too that she had been kicked on the floor, for she complained of pain in her side and kept rubbing it. When he told her he was a police-man, she said 'Thank God the police have come. Please don't leave me. I am going to die.' To be sure of her state of mind he asked her a short time later if she thought she would recover. To this she responded, 'No, dear', and with a strange assurance (as if she felt that this was the fatality which had been troubling her in the night) she insisted: 'I'm going to die, I know it.' Then he asked her what happened. Again she said, in the hearing of Skillen, Mrs Rafferty and Caughey, 'It was Robert, Robert the painter, he works for Barrett.' She added that she had spoken to him outside the bank (beside Madden's); when asked how Robert got into the house, she said that he asked to use the tele-phone and then attacked her: 'He got me by the neck and tried to choke me.'

Davis retreated to the back of Mrs Rafferty's garden to make notes on what he had seen and heard (and was strangely careful to record the motherly 'No, dear'). He joined Mrs Rafferty in the ambulance and kept vigil beside the victim's bed in hospital until 11.30 on Saturday night; against all medical expectations, she did not die until Monday evening. On arrival at the hospital, she was given morphine and a blood transfusion. A trainee nurse, Nora Heffernan, was assigned the task of re-moving the barley from her many wounds (one wound to the head and face was twelve inches long); the task was doubly dis-tressing for this young nurse, for she came from Newington Avenue and knew the victim well. The wounds were then stitched. At 7.00 pm, Mary McGowan was fully conscious again, and Davis, following instructions from his superiors, now asked her once more who attacked her. In a faint voice, but clearly, she said: 'It was Robert the painter who works for Barrett. I'm sure it was Robert. I knew him alright. It's all true.' This matches what she had said to Dr Gerald Lynch, who attended her on arrival. A Catholic who felt he had had enough of Northern Ireland's unwholesome society and would emigrate in May, Lynch was flown back from Africa in July and October so that he could tell the court: 'I knelt down to her on the stretcher and put the question to her clearly ['Who did this to you?'] and she answered quite clearly.' There was no shortage of witnesses to the victim's identification of her assailant, nor did any of them doubt the veracity of what she said.

*

After Easter Saturday, 1949, Mr Skillen would often be seen walking alone around Alexandra Park, his hands clasped behind his back, his head bent; neglected, his garden in time became a small jungle. The Rafferty twins, now in their late fifties, have never been able to speak to anyone (including the author of this book) about what they saw in the two gardens on that day. Like its implications and significance, the effects of a murder can extend much further in space and time than is commonly assumed.

11

FOR KATHLEEN, THE JOURNEY TO NEWRY was quite a pleasant event, an escape from anxieties. She was very fond of her Uncle Dan and his whitewashed farmhouse below the hills in County Down where she had spent her summer holidays as a child and the evacuation years after the blitz of April 1941. Dan was astonished when she stepped into the byre and shook his head in amusement when he heard about his sister's fears for his well-being: 'Sure nothin' ever happens down here!' They settled down to a simple lunch, talked about her father's illness, the farm, the local school teacher, the country girls who had be-friended Kathleen, their courtships and marriages. It was a brief visit, for Kathleen had to catch the district bus back into Newry in time for the Belfast bus at 2.00 pm. When she returned to Ponsonby she was bewildered by the sight of her own house and those of their immediate neighbours cordoned off, a policeman on guard, and adults and children standing around in small groups. Waiting for her, however, was Danny Casey, the twenty-year-old brother of her friends Frances and Marie. He broke the news to her gently and brought her to the Casey home, a capacious house nearby on the Antrim Road.

The Caseys were a large and jolly family, all red-haired, freckled and vigorous, and their sympathy and good spirits sus-tained her in the grim months that followed. Their father Sam was an unusually prosperous publican and they seemed the kind of family for whom everything worked out right. But the sympa-thy they extended to Kathleen and her father they too would need in time. On 2 October 1975, Marie and Frances, with their husbands, would be lined up against a wall and shot dead by Loyalist paramilitaries in a warehouse not far from where Robert lived. They were four of the 600 victims of sectarian murder that took place in North Belfast in the '70s and '80s.

Unlike the murder of Marie and Frances and their husbands, Mary McGowan's murder and its sequel – at the beginning of Ulster's 'quiet years' – would at least remain unique, perplex-ing, an isolated omen of something rotten in society; an episode dignified by association with the questionable majesty of Ulster law and its distinguished functionaries. It would not be swal-lowed up in statistics even if in its oddity it has been threatened by oblivion.

12

AT 12.20 PM ON SATURDAY, 16 April 1949, Robert the painter made his way swiftly away from Ponsonby Avenue. He crossed Halliday's Road and proceeded down the left hand side of Tiger's Bay to his girlfriend's house in Lilliput Street, a fringe street that urban development has since obliterated from the map, leaving the segregated community of Tiger's Bay more tightly bonded than ever. Practised in cool deceit, Robert had his alibi worked out in rough form before he arrived, and Lily and her married sister, Mary Erskine, just home from work as a domestic on North Circular Road, were called on to support it. He was in big trouble after a shindy with a Catholic customer and the peelers might be round asking questions. They were to say that he had been in town and called in at 12.25 to talk about wedding matters, leaving for home after about five minutes. They were to say that he gave Lily the money to buy a wedding ring and that there was nothing unusual in his appearance. There would be no wedding if they didn't stand by him.

Leaving Lilliput Street, Robert made his way across Adam Street on to lower Duncairn Gardens, and then from North Queen Street down to 13 Lower Meadow Street. Both of Robert's parents were in the kitchen when he got home at around 12.50 or 12.55. His mother, described by the police as a quiet, God-fearing woman, would decline from this day into the nervous breakdown from which she would never really recover, becoming the stupefied spectator of a suspenseful horror drama in which her lovely errant lad was the chief actor. Robert senior was a small, grey-haired man; he would be described sympathetically in the papers when the drama ended nine months later as 'a slight, white-haired figure'; yet he was resilient enough to stand by his son, whose elementary cunning was also his.

Robert probably went straight to the back yard to dispose of the gloves that had kept his fingerprints out of the McGowan home (or he might more prudently have sunk them in the static water tank he had passed on the way). He then cleaned some spots off his brightly coloured shoes (but not sufficiently to escape forensic analysis), wiped his face with a wet cloth and hung his overcoat and jacket behind the door in the front (sitting) room. Just how much of the story he told his parents at this time we can only guess at, but his father was clearly primed to say that he had returned between 12.45 and 1.00 pm, looking in no way unusual.

At 1.10 or 1.15 a long black Wolseley pulled up outside the door: very slowly, estimating the house number ('for all the world like a hearse,' said a neighbour). With rolled-up shirt sleeves and with five fresh-looking scratches on his face, Robert opened the door to District Inspector Reid (uniformed) and Detective Head Constable Thornton (plain-clothed). Both men were six-footers. In bulk as in authority they filled the little house with their presence and dwarfed the two Roberts. The twenty-one-year-old must have been daunted by the speed with which they were on to him. Moreover, Thornton, who did most of the talking, threw most Northerners, and Protestants especially, into a state of confusion until they learned, if they did, that he too was Protestant; for he was a Southerner – a Galway man – with a rich brogue, a huge contradiction as an RUC man. Yet Robert showed none of the nervousness one would have expected in the circumstances.

In soft tones which fitted neither the subject nor his virtual certainty that Robert had just committed a savage crime, Thornton explained that he was investigating a serious assault against Mrs McGowan of Ponsonby Avenue which had taken place that morning, and that he and his colleague would like to speak to Robert alone. They took him into the front room and asked him to account for his movements on that morning. He obviously realised that it would not be enough to say he was at Lily's at about 12.30 (they might believe that the attack took place earlier) and that it would be folly to mention his visit to Morrison (which signalled a desperate need for money), so he invented a plausible programme to accommodate these necessities. But it entailed two risks. He gambled that his newsagent, Robert Clarke, and his pal, Billie Booth, would not contradict claims that impinged on them. Thus he said that after breakfast at 9.45 he walked into the city, calling on the way at The Daisy in York Street for his newspaper. He then went to the back of the City Hall to see Billie Booth, who worked there as a cleaner. Booth, he said, owed him £5, which he now needed to pay for 'a taxi' for his wedding on Monday (the small sum and the single taxi were adroit). He stayed at the back of the City Hall until about 12.15 but did not see Booth. Remembering that he had arranged to call on Lily at 11.30, he said that he had boarded a Cavehill bus at the City Hall stop and arrived at Lilliput Street about 12.25 or 12.30 (which suggests that he lingered at the City Hall for a full two hours). He gave Lily the money to buy a ring and left for home at about 12.35, telling her and her sister that he had to arrange transport for the wedding.

Thornton and Reid were non-committal and left saying they would wish to interview him again shortly. They went straight to Lilliput Street, where Lily and Mary duly confirmed his account of his presence there and his perfectly normal appearance. They proceeded then to The Daisy and from there to Booth's home in Donegall Avenue. Clarke was emphatic that Robert had not collected his paper either that day or on Friday; and Booth said he had never once borrowed from Robert, had no arrangement to meet him on Saturday and did not know he was getting married. Thus Robert was tripped by his own inventiveness. Had he claimed that he was at home all morning, as his father would surely have testified, and that he was at Lily's between, say, 12.00 and 12.30, he would not have been exposed as a liar.

Obviously, however, he wanted to put as much fictional distance as possible between himself and Ponsonby on that morning.

Accompanied now by a Sergeant Hughes, Thornton got back to Meadow Street shortly before 3.00 pm, but Robert was not there; according to his sister, he had gone with his father and her husband to Houston and Williamson's. After the departure of Thornton and Reid from Lily's place at about 1.30, Mary Erskine had rushed over to Meadow Street and a family council was held with great rapidity. There was no time for recriminations and questions, though Robert may well have warned them by now that the Catholic woman with whom he had tangled might die. From the point of view of the Taylors and the Jones sisters, the McGowan affair was a case of two poor Protestant families – who between them could not scrape together £12.9s for Robert and Lily's wedding – fighting for survival against a state which owed them and their kind a very great deal; a state too which was using a smooth-talking Catholic southerner with a fancy Clark Gable moustache to lead the attack on them. It is easy enough for guilt to become victimhood and essential innocence: 'The world is not thy friend, nor the world's law.'

It was clearly thought imperative to proceed with the wedding. To abandon it might be read as an admission of guilt; in addition, and whether or not he was eventually arrested and found guilty, Mary Erskine wanted Robert to make her sister a respectable woman as soon as possible. The plan was to persuade the Williamson brothers to allow Robert's father and brother-in-law to go surety for the £12.9s, giving a written promise to pay up within two or three months; Mary played an important part in this plan and may well have devised it. Between 2.00 and 2.15 pm she and Robert entered the nearest phone box, located at the LMS railway on York Street, just opposite Morrison's pub. (It was either at this point or a little earlier that Robert decided to recruit Erskine as witness to his claim

that he visited Morrison to ask for a loan *in the afternoon*.)
Robert dialled Houston and Williamson. It was David Williamson who answered, not his brother John who had made the
original agreement. Robert put his proposal but Williamson was
taken aback and replied that it was not the custom of the firm to
enter such an agreement. But then Mary took the phone and told
him that she and her husband had hired their wedding taxis from
his firm eight months earlier and paid on the dot. If he had
checked his books at the time, Williamson would have seen that
this was a bold lie, but he did not, and the trick worked; he
agreed to give credit on the promise of surety from Robert's
father and brother-in-law. Robert promptly returned to his
home, a stone's throw away, and then he, his father and James
Connor set off for Crumlin Road, arriving at around 2.45. The
agreement was duly signed by the two guarantors and all three
left the office at approximately 3.00 pm. Outside, however,
stood two tall men, Thornton and Hughes. Robert's contest with
the law now began in earnest.

'We would like you to come with us to Glenravel Street
Barracks for further questioning, Mr Taylor,' said Thornton.
'Sure,' replied Robert, as if he was obliging them on a matter of
little consequence to himself. Thornton had encountered a wide
range of criminals in his time, but Robert disturbed and puzzled
him in a way no one else had. He was virtually certain of his
guilt but found it difficult to identify this pleasant-looking
young man with the premeditated crime whose imagery would
trouble his own sleep for decades to come. And he was amazed
at the curt if not cheeky offhandedness which Robert frequently
affected; most men in similar circumstances would have been
warily respectful, or apprehensive, or both. What would he have
to say for himself, wondered Thornton, when he was told that
Mrs McGowan had identified him in the presence of three

witnesses? Would the brittle pretence collapse and a confessional flood follow? It seemed likely.

To Hughes, the driver, Taylor seemed very small as he sat beside Thornton in the back of the Wolseley, smaller still as they led him up the steps of Glenravel Street Barracks. 'Barracks', and not 'station', as the often fortress-like police stations of that semi-colonial state were invariably called. And Glenravel was more daunting in appearance than most. Robert was taken to a whitewashed room, the walls bare but for a portrait of the King, and invited to remove his overcoat and jacket. He was then given a chair opposite the two policemen at a long oblong table under a bright light, a scenario known the world over.

Thornton spread the overcoat carefully on the table and examined it in silence, front and back; then the jacket. Saying nothing, he gestured to Hughes, lifted the coats by their loops on two rigid fingers and left the room, assigning a constable to remain with Taylor. Hughes and Thornton then drove to 13 Meadow Street to collect a complete change of clothing for Robert. They returned to find him impassive but pale, cracking his knuckles under the table. Robert had got rid of his bloody gloves, but such was the pressure of events that he had not thought to examine and dispose of the coat and jacket; it was, he now saw, a huge mistake.

'Now Robert,' said Thornton in his affable brogue, 'if you wouldn't mind changing into these clothes we've brought you?'

'Sure.'

As he undressed, they noticed that he wore two vests and two pairs of socks.

'In weather like this?' asked Hughes, 'One of the cold-blooded sort, eh?'

Robert did not appreciate the barbed jest: 'It's cold in our house at night. We can't all afford big fires like some people.'

At this point, Thornton abruptly asked Robert to lift his right foot on to the chair. He then produced a piece of white paper and a pocket knife, and proceeded to scrape a large patch of dried blood from Robert's ankle and another from his instep, letting the powder fall into an envelope. Robert was now allowed to dress and the questioning began.

Asked about his movements before 12.30, he gave the same account as before, insisting in particular that he had not been near Antrim Road, Atlantic Avenue or Ponsonby Avenue that morning. Then the questions moved closer to the crime. What was his financial situation? Hughes had searched his pockets and found four shillings and two pence, an empty wallet and the letter from Houston and Williamson demanding £12.9s. by that day at the latest. 'Unemployed, hard up, desperate for cash, eh?' asked Hughes. Robert 'muttered' (the term is Hughes's) that he did have money. In the morning he had £4 left from what he had saved in the post office. But he gave £3.10s to his fiancée to buy a ring, he paid his sister 5s. which he owed her and spent some of the rest on a newspaper and tram fares. This fitted well with his alleged comings and goings and gave the impression of honest accounting. But he would have known that it did not dispose of the implications of the letter. Hence the 'muttered' response.

This issue led to the next question: Did he know Mrs McGowan of Ponsonby Avenue? Here he was cool candour itself, almost voluble. Yes, he did know her. He had worked for her several times. Her husband owned a pub in town called The Waldorf. The last time he worked for her was at least twelve months ago and he hadn't seen her since. He worked for three or four days that time but didn't like it. She was always complaining about his work and he had asked the boss to get him off the job. 'Did you know she had a telephone?' asked Thornton (less a question than an attempt to unnerve). Yes he did; when he was painting there his mate 'used to phone the boss for stuff'. Asked if Mrs McGowan called him Bobby or Bob or Rob, he replied, 'She always called me Robert.' Thornton and Hughes exchanged looks and said nothing.

Thornton's silent removal of the blood from his foot and his allusion to the telephone excuse might have been enough in the circumstances to undo any young man's confidence and lead quickly to a confession of guilt. But Robert's frank admission that he knew there was a telephone, even though that instrument was bonded to his crime, nicely sustained the pretence of innocence. What followed, however, was much more testing. Thornton brought the overcoat, socks and trousers and laid them out carefully on the long table, almost like an outfitter obliging a customer. He sat down, leaned back in his chair and – I reconstruct the exchange from Thornton's summary account in court – said to the suspect:

'Now Robert, we have a problem here about blood. First of all, there are those scratches on your face. Am I right, Sergeant Hughes, in thinking there are five of them and that they look quite fresh? I am? Well now Robert, would you mind telling us how you got them?'

As if it had been a question of no significance, Robert replied:

'It could have been my sister's youngster done it when I was playing with him.'

'I see,' said Thornton, 'a remarkably aggressive child, eh? Well, then, about these reddish stains on your clothes: to be precise, on the right sleeve of your overcoat, on the knees and the left turn-up of your trousers, and the ankle and instep of your double sock. Take a good look and tell me if you agree that they are bloodstains. Take your time, but don't touch them please, some are still damp.'

Robert glanced quickly at the stains and said, 'That's not blood, that's paint.'

Thornton touched the largest stain with his little finger and stamped it on the table:

'I'm no expert, but I'd say it was blood. However, we'll let the forensic scientists settle that one – and tell us the blood group of the owner into the bargain. But what about the stuff I scraped off your instep and your ankle? Was that paint and if so, how did it get there through two pairs of socks? And why, if it was paint, was it easy for me to scrape it off?'

There was no answer to these questions. Robert shrugged his shoulders and arched his mouth as if to say, 'I've no idea.' A long silence was broken by a constable who called Thornton to the phone. It was a message from the Antrim Road Barracks telling him that a Mrs Shiels of 28 Ponsonby Avenue had come forward with a statement to the effect that she had seen Robert on Atlantic Avenue a few minutes after 12.00 noon; she knew him well and he had done work for her too. There was also a message at the desk from Davis at the Mater Hospital reporting Mrs McGowan's reiterated assertion that 'Robert did it, Robert the painter who works for Barrett.'

An hour later Robert was asked to write a statement summarising all he had said; this he did, and signed with a flourish. Later that evening Thornton went to his cell and told him he was charging him with the attempted murder of Mary McGowan. When asked if he had anything to say to the charge, and duly cautioned that it might be used in evidence in court, he replied airily: 'Just say I'm innocent, that's all.'

*

Seventy-year-old Mary Shiels was something of a busybody, an observant window watcher who was apt to remember the names of the lads who carelessly kicked a ball into her garden or played tricks with her door knocker on Halloween night. She did not resent being approached by Head Constable Thornton after mass on Easter Sunday morning and courteously asked if she would accompany him in the big car to an identification parade in Glenravel Street Barracks. Apart from the fact that she was naturally glad to help the police in their efforts to bring Mrs McGowan's assailant to justice, she quite enjoyed her temporary metamorphosis into a figure of public importance. At the parade, she was asked to pick out from the twelve men before her the one she saw on Atlantic Avenue on Saturday. She went straight to Robert and said, 'That's him.' As he was led back to his cell, Robert remarked to Sergeant Hughes, 'That woman knows me well.' He may have thought the remark would subtly suggest that she was being spitefully sectarian, but of course her knowing him well strengthened the case against him.

Robert had long hours in his cell for the enormity of what he had done to sink in and overwhelm him: a quiet, clean strangulation had become an inhuman mess which none of his previous misdemeanours remotely resembled. He had time also to brood on the ominous burden of Thornton's questions, on the certainty that the stains would be shown to be blood (and from Mary McGowan's blood group) and on the possibility that Mrs Shiels had seen him in or near Ponsonby on Saturday morning. There was also the problem as to whether Booth and Clarke would concur with what he said about them. Nevertheless, his self-confidence did not collapse; nor did his determination to avoid confessing to the crime weaken; not even when he was driven handcuffed up Crumlin Road and through the huge gates of the ugliest gaol in Ireland.

He had spent twenty-four hours alone in his prison cell when, on Monday night, Thornton returned to tell him that Mrs McGowan had died and that he was now charging him with murder. Asked again if he had anything to say to the charge, he responded (it is remarkable how the flavour of personality comes through in the recorded phrases of a policeman's note-

book): 'Still innocent.' Asked if he wanted to be represented at
the postmortem, he shrugged his shoulders and said: 'It's alright.' That his cockiness persisted may have been due to the
fact that he had already thought up for his defence lawyers a
more plausible explanation than paint for those stains. Luck too
would favour him in the matter of blood grouping: Mary
McGowan's blood group was 'O', but so was his. 'Never say
die' might have been his motto.

13

ALTHOUGH ITS HARSH SECTARIAN divide is more conspicuous than ever today, Belfast is now a vibrant and attractive
city, offering an abundance of cultural diversions. Except for
those who experienced it, however, nothing more colourless
than life in Belfast in the late 1940s can be imagined. It was
about then that the joke began to circulate in the South: first
prize, one week in Belfast, second prize, two weeks. The joke
was resented, but many knew in their hearts that it was bitter
truth in jest.

The war and its excitements were over. The great empty
spaces left by the German air raids in the city centre and beyond
remained and figured a deeper emptiness. The romantic Ameri-
can servicemen had gone: their accents, their glamorous uni-
forms, their prodigal giving and spending, and their easy charm
had temporarily transformed the atmosphere of the city, so that
their departure left a void in the imagination of women and boys
(the men were glad to see the back of them). For the majority,
the height of entertainment was a night at the pictures, enduring
mostly third-rate movies, perhaps after queueing in the cold for
an hour or more. For men, there was also football in bleak stadi-
ums, the dogs, the sawdusted pub; for married women, church
activities in abundance and the restricted menu of the BBC's

Light Programme and Home Service. No television, no transistor radios, no LPs, no CDs; nor had bingo arrived. Only a small minority possessed a car, foreign travel was a singular novelty and, for most of those who could afford them, holidays were a week or two on the wind-swept promenades of Bangor and Portrush. Petrol was rationed and clothes were rationed. So was food. Christmas parcels from the South were opened by the customs to remove sugar and chocolate. And intensifying the drabness and meanness of it all were the pervasive, contending puritanisms of Ulster Protestantism and Irish Catholicism.

The anti-partition election was a phoney war, an assertion that nothing had changed or would change. The slow, unsensational process of post-war reconstruction in Britain and Europe dominated the newspapers. Sensational murders, like sex scandals, were mostly what happened in England, and Ulster newspapers gave them scant attention. Before 1949, the last person to be executed in Northern Ireland had been a nineteen-year-old IRA 'man', Tom Williams, who had killed a policeman in a shoot-out that began as an attempt to draw the RUC away from a banned Easter Rising march: not premeditated, not shocking, not mysterious. Yet the court was filled for the trial and its drama extended to the streets. Outside the Crumlin Road Gaol at the time of the hanging, a crowd of about two hundred women and girls burst into 'God save the King', while on the other side of the street between twenty and thirty Republican women knelt in prayer. The national anthem was followed by cheers; then 'Land of Hope and Glory' and 'There'll always be an England' were sung, while the women opposite remained on their knees. But that was in 1942 and even then the drama of the event was dwarfed by the news that came in every day about devastating air raids on England and the losing struggle with the Germans on sea and land.

By contrast, the case of Robert the Painter, occurring in the dull post-election period of 1949, became a judicial drama of nine months' duration, during which time, as Lord Chief Justice Porter said in the Appeal Court in January 1950, 'The topic was on everybody's lips.' The case was not sectarian or political in the obvious sense, but it had teasing implications of that kind. After the election, the murder of a Catholic woman by a young Protestant from a well-known Loyalist ghetto inevitably induced an alignment of sympathies and prejudices and raised in the minds of many the question: Would justice be done? Recalling recently his own coverage of part of the second trial for *The Belfast Telegraph*, John Cole commented on his innocence in failing to see the sectarian dimension of the case, explaining that he was twenty-one at the time and much more interested then in socialism than sectarianism. Yet the Lord Chief Justice, the judge in the second trial, was addressing what was in the mind of many when he said in his charge to the jury:

> Set aside any feelings that there is the slightest religious issue or prejudice which anyone outside the court may have endeavoured to introduce into the case. You shall deal with it as a sordid social crime. It matters not to me what the religion of the accused or the victim may be. As long as I preside in these courts, I will see that Catholics, Protestants, Jews, Moslems, or Hindus will receive from me and this court British justice.

The judge's grandiose allusion to 'other' religions was the source of much wry comment. Said Mrs Ned Gibbons's friend, Mrs Sharkey, on their way home from the trial: 'As if we didn't know what everything boils down to in this lovely wee town of ours!'

But even more likely to command public attention than the sectarian dimension of the case was the singularly brutal nature of the killing and the contrasting appearance and demeanour of the alleged killer. And the imputed motive, too, which seemed grotesquely incommensurate with the crime: money to pay for taxis and carnations. Even the detectives involved were sometimes troubled by the seemingly improbable nature of what they saw as the plain facts of the case.

Between April and December the papers provided a steady flow of information on the case and with a degree of repetition that fixed the details of the story in the public imagination. On the morning of Monday, 18 April, *The News-Letter* carried a brief item – a three-inch column – announcing that a man would appear that day in the Belfast Custody Court charged with the attempted murder of Mrs Mary McGowan of Ponsonby Avenue. Her screams, it was said, had been heard by her neighbours who then found her lying in her garden with severe injuries to head and body. Her attacker had gained access by knocking on the door and asking to use her telephone; she was now dangerously ill in the Mater Hospital (a location which signalled to the reader that she was a Catholic). The Tuesday morning accounts of Monday's proceedings stretched to over five inches and gave Robert's name and address (in effect his religion too) as well as his age and occupation. Head Constable Thornton's evidence and the young man's response tersely but vividly projected for the reader the horrific nature and the radical incompatibilities of the case. 'It was evident', the paper reported Thornton as saying, that Taylor 'had tried to strangle her, a cord being tied round her neck. Her mouth and throat were cut, and lumps of flesh were cut out as if with a knife. Both her eyes were closed and a pot of boiling soup . . . had been thrown over her'.

Thornton reported that when charged and asked if he had anything to say, Taylor had replied: 'Just say I am innocent, that's all.' And when asked in court by the magistrate if he had anything to say before being remanded in custody, he replied coolly: 'I was nowhere near the district.' The nature of the crime imputed to the young man and the clarity and firmness of his denials (suggesting the calmness of perfect innocence), combined at this stage to make a case that many found baffling as well as shocking. Surely something was wrong here? Had the police blundered? Should they not be looking for someone easily identifiable as a violent maniac? A grubby and wild-eyed escapee from a secure unit in one of the Ulster asylums? It seemed inconceivable that an ordinary, pleasant young man could be capable of so savage a crime: the routine barbarism of Loyalists and Republicans in the 1970s and after had yet to educate people on the worst potentialities of human nature.

The papers reported three more appearances for Taylor in court for the purpose of keeping him on remand. These whetted the appetite for the papers' lengthy accounts of the three-day hearing which started on 30 May in a special court. Here the police outlined for the resident magistrate the case against the accused – a preliminary justification for sending him to the Crown Court for trial on the charge of murder. All seats were filled in this court on the first day, and on the second day all standing room was taken up as well, while many people were turned away. Before a huge audience, the drama of the boy in the open-necked shirt had started in earnest.

The Crown prosecutor called upon a long list of witnesses. Even with the deliberate exclusion of evidence from one major witness (the dead woman) the case against Taylor seemed conclusive. The account he gave to the police of his movements on the morning of 16 April was shown to be riddled with lies clearly designed to put them off his track: his last visit to McGowans had been two and not, as he had claimed, twelve or more months earlier; he *was* in the district that morning; he did *not* call at The Daisy to collect his *Irish News*; his friend Billie Booth did *not* owe him money. Moreover, he had crucially omitted to mention that he had called on Morrison on the morning of the assault and failed to extract from him a loan of £20 to cover his wedding expenses. Then there was forensic evidence connecting him with the crime: blood, hairs, fibres. Only a miracle, it seemed, could save him.

The assistant defence lawyer, Mr J. Fox, put a few perfunctory questions to the witnesses. In one of these he astutely sought to fix 'Bobby' in the minds of the public and the jurors-to-be as Taylor's first name. Were any of the other painters who worked for your mother called 'Bobby?', he asked Kathleen. It did not matter to him that she replied in the negative and said that she and her mother only knew him as 'Robert'. The jury would probably assume that these people didn't know the real Taylor, Bobby to his friends, innocent Bobby, bubbly Breen's lookalike.

The public were tantalised by the revelation that evidence from a key witness was excluded from the hearing. At the start of proceedings on the first day, brief reference was made to a statement taken by the police from Mary McGowan before her death in the Mater Hospital; and the second day's proceedings began with a wrangle on this matter between the prosecution and defence lawyers, the latter claiming that the words of the dying woman had to be ruled out as inadmissible because they were not uttered in the presence of Taylor himself and so could not be challenged. The magistrate certainly was of the opinion that publication of this evidence 'would have a serious effect' and ruled that its admissibility or otherwise would have to be decided at the High Court, a decision as disappointing to the defence, who wanted it ruled out once and for all, as it was gratifying to the prosecution. Of course to those who lived in Newington and Tiger's Bay, by contrast with the public at large, the substance of the evidence in question was no mystery. On the night of 16 April it was buzzed all around Newington that

Mrs McGowan had named her attacker as Robert, the painter who worked for Barrett of Sunnyside Street; and from Barrett himself all Tiger's Bay soon learned the same. But these people too had to wait to see if the victim's devastating statement would be taken into account; and they would wait in suspense, knowing that the law often works in ways unpredictable and mysterious to ordinary folk.

The trial proper was to begin at the end of July, an event anticipated with considerable anxiety by the Catholics of Newington, fearful as they were of what might erupt if Taylor, as was right, were found guilty. The signs were not good. After the hearing in June the houses of Mrs Rafferty, Mr Skillen and Mrs Shiels were barracked by angry groups from Tiger's Bay shouting 'Fenian liars' and the like. On the Twelfth, an unusually large and noisy parade made its way down Ponsonby and around Newington, banging on the Lambegs and singing 'Dolly Brae' more lustily than ever before.

14

BEFORE 16 APRIL 1949, Robert Taylor's parents saw their younger son as restless and a bit troublesome, but assumed he would settle down in time. When he was charged with murder, they were stunned and quite unable to comprehend what had happened. While the mother withdrew into the silence of deep depression, the father told himself and his friends that 'up in Ponsonby things must have somehow just got out of hand' and sought to help Robert avoid the consequences of the fatality which engulfed him. He was doubtless sincere when in the midst of his perjuries in court he said that his son was a good boy and that he never knew him to be violent.

What does a little man, a mere labourer, do in a situation such as that which confronted Robert Taylor senior? If he belongs to a tight-knit community, he turns to its Men In The Know, its elders. First, a Catholic solicitor, Anthony Lunn, was recommended; surprising, but the Orangeman's view was that Catholic solicitors in the North had a lot more experience than their Protestant colleagues in dealing with criminal charges and the police. But most important of all, of course, was finding the right sort of barrister. The man recommended was George Boyle Hanna, KC. He had a fine political pedigree, was a very clever advocate and was clearly on the way up. His father, also George Boyle Hanna, had been a Unionist MP from 1919 until 1937, and then a County Court judge; in 1922 he had complained that the new Special Powers Act designed to control Nationalist unrest was too complicated and recommended a draconian simplicity in the wording: 'The Home Secretary [Minister of Home Affairs] shall have the power to do what he likes, or let somebody else do what he likes for him.' The legendary status of the Reverend 'Roaring' Hugh Hanna, whose sectarian rhetoric at Orange rallies and marches gave rise in the 1870s to many riots, was not to George Boyle's or his son's political and professional disadvantage. George junior, now aged forty-three, had been Commissioner for the Ulster Unionists in Armagh from 1934 to 1941, was still active in the party as in the Order, and was known to have political ambitions.

But would he accept the case? The layman would assume that the ghastly nature of the crime and Taylor's obvious guilt would deter any intelligent lawyer with a modicum of moral sensibility and professional prudence. However, a defending counsel's role precludes liking or disliking, approving or disapproving of his client; it requires that he accept his client's plea and challenge the evidence assembled against it by the prosecution. Hanna may well have loathed this brutal and smoothly unrepentant young killer. But a brilliant defence of the indefensible, even if it fails, always wins professional respect for the lawyer from his peers. A spirited defence of Taylor, moreover, could only improve Hanna's political prospects; indeed, to refuse the challenge might well have had the reverse effect.

Hanna's task as defending counsel to Taylor was rendered especially difficult by the fact that the prosecuting counsel appointed to the case was Lancelot Curran, KC, MP. Here was a barrister with an impressive history, appearance and character. He had fought with distinction in two world wars (rising to the rank of major), was a Unionist MP since 1945 and Attorney General since 1947, the youngest in Ulster history. Tall, handsome, severe and cold, he was renowned for the incisiveness of his cross-examinations. He was seven years older than the affable Hanna and would outlive him by twenty years. Like Hanna's, his career would make a sudden leap forward immediately after the second Taylor trial; yet his posthumous reputation would be darkened when his mysterious behaviour in the case of his daughter's murder in 1952, which resulted in a scandalous miscarriage of justice, was belatedly made public. (The connection between the two most notorious murder cases in Ulster's legal history is stranger than fiction; but more of that anon.)

The case of the Crown versus Robert Taylor opened on 25 July and lasted four days. The defence had exercised their right to raise objections to the composition of the jury, so that of the twelve persons initially chosen, three men who had obviously Catholic surnames and two women were withdrawn, and what seemed like a fully Protestant male group was formed. Had the case been that of a Catholic standing trial for the murder of a Protestant, the same procedure would, of course, have been employed: neither side had a monopoly on suspicion and distrust.

The court was packed, both the gallery and the ground floor; the police had difficulty in controlling the queues outside and dismissing the disappointed who cluttered the entrance hall and the high steps of the great building. The heated sectarian atmosphere of an Ulster July as well as the June hearing gave an intense expectancy to the event; yet many who were drawn to the court might not have acknowledged the sectarian ingredient in their preoccupation with the case. Few men could take time off work to attend a trial, so most of those present were women, students (especially law students), the retired and the unemployed.

When all the seats had been filled and standing room taken up, the jury filed in and took their seats, followed by the judge and the accused. During the hum that prevailed before Mr Pollock, the Clerk of the Crown and Peace, called for silence and opened the proceedings, Mrs Gibbons (who had spotted the Tiger's Bay grocer) leaned over to Mrs Sharkey and whispered:

'Would you look who's on the jury! First on the right. Looks like he's the foreman.'

'Well, well, well. Who's in luck, I ask you?'

In his opening remarks, Judge Sheil went out of his way to explain that throughout the trial the jury would not be allowed to separate or mix with the public and that accommodation and meals would be provided for them by the police inside the court house. The ban on physical separation in murder cases – standard legal requirement in Northern Ireland at that time – would become an issue of immense significance in the second trial. It is worth noting that it was given emphasis at the outset of the Crown's protracted endeavour to find Taylor guilty and punish him for his crime.

When the charge against him was read out, and throughout most of the first day's proceedings, Taylor sat unperturbed in the dock, glancing occasionally to his left where some of his friends were seated. His apparent calmness, his neat appearance, nicely groomed wavy hair and immaculate, open-necked shirt – signs of Hanna's directorial skills – all conspired to engender disbelief as one witness after another was called upon to describe what he had allegedly done.

Before calling his witnesses, Curran gave a lucid summary of the prosecution case, omitting however all reference to the murdered woman's dying statement. He described her movements on Saturday morning, the injuries inflicted on her, the interventions of her neighbours Mr Skillen, Mrs Rafferty and Mr Caughey, the prompt arrival of the police and her death from her injuries on Monday evening. He explained why she was alone on Easter Saturday, pointed out that money was the obvious motive for the assault (the ransacked handbag, case and drawers), and told of the visit paid by the police to Taylor's home within forty-five minutes of the assault (since he excluded reference to Mary McGowan's identification of her assailant, he could not explain why suspicion fell instantly on Taylor).

He described the stains on Taylor's clothes, his claim that those on his coat and trousers were paint and his inability to account for the blood on his sock and foot. Advancing on the evidence given at the hearing, he said that all these stains had now been forensically examined and identified as fresh blood of group O – Mary McGowan's group (but fortunately for Robert, his too). Moreover, forensic analysis had found white, blood-stained hairs on Taylor's clothing which tallied with those of Mrs McGowan, fibres on his shoes matching those from her carpet and traces of Lyons's wax shoe polish on the soles of her shoes, the kind used by Taylor and his family and not used by the McGowans.

Finally, he explained that the evidence of the witnesses to be called would show that Taylor had lied in his account of where and how he spent the morning on the day of the assault; it would show too that he had made an unsuccessful bid for the loan of £20 on that morning. The crown, he said, did not have to establish a motive, but if one were necessary it was obvious: Taylor's desperation on that particular day for money to cover his wedding expenses.

Curran rounded off by emphasising the obvious import of 'the cold logical facts' of the case and the need to look at them 'dispassionately'. In this he may have been revealing something of his own temperament, but primarily he was motivated by an awareness of the extent to which emotion could sway the jury: on the one hand, tribal or sectarian feeling and, on the other, instinctive horror at the thought of this attractive young man with the open-necked shirt being taken to the gallows and hung by the neck until dead.

Which is why Curran called Kathleen McGowan as his first witness, a young person of exactly the same age as Taylor. As was customary at that time for the bereaved, she was dressed in mourning black and would remain so until twelve months had elapsed since her mother's death. Asked if she recognised the accused, she turned to her right where he sat in the dock, looked at him briefly (he did not return her look) and replied, 'Yes, that is Robert the painter.' She then testified that he had worked for her mother four times and had called at their house in mid-February. The rest of her evidence contributed nothing of 'logical' value to the case, but its emotional value was great: it initiated Curran's very successful attempt to emphasise the horrific nature of the crime committed by Taylor. One would like to think that he had apologised in advance to Kathleen for what he subjected her to here, but neither in court nor in private did he do so; in fact he never once spoke privately to her in either of the two trials, the only sympathetic words she received coming from his junior counsel, Mr W.F. McCoy, KC. At Curran's request, a grim array of objects was produced and brought forward to Kathleen for identification, one by one: the spanner ('No, we had no spanner in our house'), the bent carving knife ('I saw my mother use it to cut bread that morning'; 'No, it was not bent then'); the soup pot ('Yes, it is ours'); a torn, blood-stained dress ('Yes, it was my mother's'); photographs of her mother's bruised, scalded and wounded body taken by Sergeant R.J. Fitzsimons after her death ('Yes . . . my mother'). Her quiet demeanour in all of this seemed to signify a rare self-control, but in fact it was a form of numbness: she would remember the whole experience of those months as one of shock, bewilderment and isolation.

She was briefly cross-examined by Hanna's junior counsel, Mr J. Fox. This barrister she actually found sympathetic, for he spoke to her about her mother and got her to agree that she was 'a generous, large-hearted type of woman and a good, devout, practising Catholic'. She did not realise, however, that his description of her mother as generous and large-hearted was a sly way of distracting attention from his desire to establish that she was a woman deeply committed to the rites of the Catholic church, a fact which Hanna had decided to use to the prosecution's disadvantage. Nevertheless, it was a mistake on Fox's part to acknowledge the murdered woman's natural goodness, not because it made the crime seem more heinous, for the defence itself intended to agree that it was horrible, but because it introduced a contradiction to the extraordinary argument which Hanna would concoct in order to discredit Mary McGowan's statement that it was Robert who attacked her. Fox's error was compounded by his cross-examination of the next witness, the bread-server Bernard McKeever. He was partly responsible for the one memorable element in McKeever's replies, namely his insistence that 'Mrs McGowan was a very nice lady'. The breadman looked at the jury and all round the court when he said that. It seemed to be all he was interested in saying to anyone: 'She was a very nice lady.'

The lady's neighbour and friend Robert Skillen appeared next in the witness box and then the journalist John Caughey. Both men gave an exact account of what they saw and did when Mrs McGowan's cries were heard, Caughey stressing that although he knew her for twenty years, he did not recognise her at that moment. Both omitted reference to her naming of Robert the painter as the assailant; for Curran had decided that that, if admissible, should come up in the evidence given by Mrs Rafferty, Detective Sergeant Davis and the hospital doctor. Had DNA analysis been available to the prosecution, or if Taylor's fingerprints had been found at the scene of the crime, the case against him could have been decided without reference to Mary McGowan's naming of 'Robert the painter who worked for Barrett'. In the circumstances, her evidence was damning and Hanna was desperate to have it excluded. Indeed his argument that it should be ignored moved beyond ingenuity and exaggeration in the direction of slander and absurdity. It provided a distant, forensic parallel to Robert's crisis in that it showed how desperation will push a man into an extremity which neither he himself nor anyone else would have expected him to occupy.

In order to settle the question, the judge delayed resumption of the trial proceedings after lunch and for almost two hours listened to the contending arguments of defence and prosecution as to the testimonial validity of the dying woman's words. Curran's argument was that although the statement identifying Taylor was made by someone who could not be cross-examined, a normal requirement in law, nevertheless there were precedents and rulings which showed that the evidence of a person who knew that he or she was dying could be entertained. Mary McGowan believed and believed rightly that she was going to die; she had named her assailant quite explicitly and in the presence of witnesses; furthermore, as a deeply religious and a good woman at the point of death she would not have named Taylor maliciously. Hanna, however, contended that 'she did not believe that death was imminent', that the evidence showed that all her thoughts were of a purely 'terrestrial' kind. 'She did not ask that any message should be sent to her husband, there was no evidence of any farewell, she did not make any arrangements for her funeral or her affairs.' If her thoughts had been about the afterlife she would not have said 'Phone Mick at the shop' or 'Thank God the police are here'. Furthermore – Hanna clearly thought this was his most telling point – she did not ask for a priest to administer the last rites, which is what a devout Catholic would surely have done if she believed she was dying.

Then, however, he overstepped the mark of reason and decency, and in doing so made a nonsense of his assistant's recognition that Mrs McGowan was a generous, large-hearted woman and the breadman's claim that she was 'a very nice lady': 'I suggest that the words ['Robert did it. Robert the painter', etc.] were dictated by feelings of anger or desire for revenge.' Then he cited at length the case of *R. v. Abbott* (1903) as a reminder to the judge that the evidence of a dead person 'should be approached scrupulously and with almost superstitious care'. With a mildly ironic allusion to Hanna's solemn phrasing, Judge Sheil responded that he was doing just that, and that having weighed both arguments carefully he was ruling that the statement must be admitted. Like Curran, he found it impossible to accept that the lady did not believe she was dying when in fact she insisted several times that she was. He might have commented on the absurdity of the idea that a woman in mortal agony should make arrangements for her funeral. He might have observed that the fact that her last thoughts were not about herself but about the distress her death would cause others was by no means inconsistent with a devout Catholicism; and that as a good-living woman she would have had no cause to be anxious about the afterlife and instantly call for the Last Rites (which were duly administered in the hospital anyhow). Perhaps he was too kindly to subject the learned KC to the intellectual humiliation his arguments invited. But having failed to sway the judge with his sophistries, Hanna did not intend to abandon them; he must have recognised them for what they were, but the case was desperate and he would try by every means in his cross-questioning to elicit some scrap of evidence to support them; and in due time he would hammer them into the ears of the jury.

After this discussion (unheard of course by the jurymen and the public), the trial was resumed and Mrs Rafferty was called to the stand. She was directed by Curran's careful questions to recount in full detail the events of the morning when Robert had rendered her friend unrecognisable; nothing was left to the imagination. Curran's questioning completed, Hanna was asked if he wished to cross-examine the witness, and apparently for mere form's sake he did so. He was understandably deflated by the failure of his strenuous efforts to move the judge, and what Mrs Rafferty had just said made his whole task seem impossible. Not surprisingly, he was at a loss about where to go: the few questions he put to her led nowhere, merely invited her to repeat what she had said already and were even counterproductive. Some law students who had come to see Ulster's leading advocates at work on a high priority case were not impressed by his floundering:

'There was a good deal of blood coming from Mrs McGowan?'

'Yes. There was a good deal lying on the ground.'

'Did you hear her screaming?'

'No.'

'She didn't ask you to send a message to her husband?'

'She said: "Poor Daddy, this will be a terrible shock to him".'

'Thank you. That will be all.'

Judge Sheil made matters worse for Hanna by intervening at this point with a few questions for Mrs Rafferty:

'Did she complain of anything else in addition to the attempt to choke her and the pouring of soup on her?'

'She said that he beat her.'

'At what stage did she say that happened?'

'He beat her and then he threw soup over her.'

'And kicked her?'

'Yes.'

There was a pause here and an audible silence in the court. The judge could be heard taking a deep breath, as of an old man wearied by a lifetime listening to tales of human wickedness. But directly below and confronting him in the dock the pleasant countenance of the young man accused was clearly saying: 'This has nothing to do with me.'

Mrs Rafferty was followed in the witness stand by Detective Sergeant Davis, no partisan neighbour or co-religionist, but an earnest, plain-speaking detective whose evidence gave hers a cast-iron validity. He described Mary McGowan's shocking appearance and the disordered state of the house when he arrived, and explained that twice in Ponsonby and once in the hospital he had heard her say who assaulted her. The first day's proceedings ended with this exchange between him and Curran:

'When she arrived at the hospital did you remain at her bedside?'

'Yes, until 11.30 at night.'

'Did she speak at any time?'

'At about 7.00 pm she said that Robert beat her in the hall. I asked her if she was sure that it was Robert beat her, and she replied: "I am sure it was Robert. I knew him alright; it is all true."'

'What condition was she in at that time?'

'She was very weak.'

'Was her voice strong?'

'No.'

'Was she quite conscious?'

'Yes.'

Curran resumed his place at the bench and waited. A pause, then the judge looked at the clock and rose to go. Robert was led underground by two wardens and back to his cell via the tunnel connecting the Courthouse and the Gaol at the opposite side of the road. Then the jury rose, the lawyers and the journalists at their respective tables gathered their papers, and the people made their way out, not in a babble of voices, but with a great shuffle, murmuring guardedly to one another in pairs and small groups.

There is a fictional narrative where, in a case like this, and at such a point as this, the defence lawyer dismays everyone by suddenly walking away from his brief: either because he is appalled by what he is attempting to negate, or because he knows that he faces defeat, or because he is overcome by a generalised disgust at the profession he has chosen; or for two or all of these reasons combined (the exact nature of his motivation is difficult to determine). But so far as is known, such a story has yet to be written; and although the layman might forgive him if he did, Hanna was not the man to disgrace his profession or honour his humanity in that way. The first day had begun badly for him, but he would be back on the morrow gamely committed to the task of making black white and white black.

15

THERE WAS AGAIN KEEN PUBLIC INTEREST in the case and queues formed outside the court before the trial commenced', wrote *The Irish News* concerning the second day of the trial. But these polite objective phrases hardly catch the atmosphere among the people assembled on the steps on that warm July morning ('Good Fenian crop in the soil', 'Hell would be too good for him', 'How on earth can Hanna do anything with this job?'). Nor do the journalist's words touch on the way minds were variously affected by the proximity and the contrast

between the elegant Courthouse – with its classical portico and
colonnade and its towering statue of a handsome Justice and her
scales – and the squat ugly building of the Gaol staring up at it
from across the road, as if eager to bury its next victim in quick-
lime, as it had buried young Tom Williams before him. For
some, the contrast imaged the two inseparable aspects of Law;
for others, its appearance and its reality.

The public would now hear Hanna's attempts to find some
cracks, something to cling to, in the evidence for the prosecution
presented on the previous day by Detective Sergeant Davis and
today by Dr Lynch (who tended to Mary McGowan in the hospital), by Dr J.A. Johnston, the pathologist, and (at great length)
by Head Constable Thornton. Lynch's evidence included his
statement that Mrs McGowan had named Taylor as the assailant, but consisted mainly of a meticulous description of her injuries. His clinical style added to the horror of what had been sub-
jectively described by other witnesses and reminded Kathleen of
the stark photographs she had been asked to look at on the previous day and would spend a lifetime trying to forget:

> She was suffering from extensive laceration to the
> skull, which took the form of multiple incised
> wounds. These could have been caused by a knife or
> a broken bottle. There was a large wound and several
> incised wounds on the head, also an incised wound to
> the right ear and an incised wound near the mouth.
> She was bleeding from the mouth and both ears, and
> her nose was fractured. Her face was swollen, her lips
> bluish and both eyes closed. Her tongue was swollen.
> There was a small wound on the right hand and left
> forefinger. There were bruises on the back and to
> both hands and her neck. There were extensive burns
> to the face and neck and both arms. There were
> bruises on the legs. The cause of death was secondary
> shock, the result of having received multiple bruises,

severe loss of blood, severe burns, aggravated by attempted strangulation.

The pathologist who conducted the post-mortem had nothing
of note to add to this, other than that Mrs McGowan was a
woman with sandy, slightly greying hair, of somewhat small
stature, but well nourished, and that the bruising on forehead,
lips and chin was 'enormous'. But Thornton spent more than an
hour recounting his visit to the McGowan home, his questioning
and arrest of Robert, the latter's answers and comments, and Mrs
Shiels's and Robert's responses to the identification parade. He
also read out Robert's formal statement with its emphatic conclusion: 'I was not on the Antrim Road, Atlantic Avenue or Ponsonby Avenue today. I did not call at Mrs McGowan's today.'

Hanna's cross-questioning seemed again to be aimless if not
counterproductive for a while. Then it became desperate. A major difficulty for him was the way in which Davis's evidence
and Mrs Rafferty's were mutually supportive: if only he had
been able to insinuate that she was predictably and necessarily
biased, likely to turn her own suspicions into fact! He came near
to that by hinting that she had fed Davis the information about
Mary McGowan's statements. Precisely when, he asked Davis,
did he make his entries on this matter in his notebook? Did he
not make his entries 'correspond' with the evidence of Mrs
Rafferty subsequent to his first visit to the house? Davis flushed
and retorted that he was 'telling the story as fairly and as
straight and honestly as I could'. Hanna, however, would not
concede defeat here, but darkly asked that the detective's notebook be made an exhibit in the case; as if careful scrutiny would
justify what he was hinting at.

But he would not return to this audacious line of attack; instead, he attempted to discredit the most important witness of all,
thinking no doubt that if he could do that then the detective's evidence would be irrelevant. Said he to Dr Johnston: 'Would you

expect a woman who had been subjected to such a violent attack
to be hysterical?' The pathologist was not helpful: 'No. I would
not. But she would obviously be excited.' But Hanna would not
be put off this line of argument. Despite her compassionate concern while in extreme pain for others, Mary McGowan would
become in his presentation a woman rendered angry, vengeful
and unhinged by the assault. As yet however he had merely
placed the seed of that idea in the minds of the jury (who had not
heard what he said to the judge in their absence after lunch when
the admissibility of her evidence was debated).

The third day of the trial was marked by an even more intense public interest than before. Long queues began to form
two hours before the court opened; favoured by the good
weather, many of those who did not gain entrance remained outside all day, while a large number of those who did get in had
come equipped with attaché cases filled with sandwiches and
drinks and stayed inside at lunch time in case they would lose
their seats. The big attraction of the day was that the prosecution
would be completed and the defence case would begin, with
Taylor being put in the witness stand.

Prosecution witness Dr J.B. Firth, a Home Office Forensic
scientist brought over from Preston, confirmed what Curran had
said about the evidence found on Taylor's clothing and explained that the bloodstained hairs matching those of Mrs
McGowan were fifteen in number and were located at the top of
his overcoat (where they would have lodged when he grappled
with her). He was also insistent that 'the material on the soles of
the deceased's shoes could only have been that of Lyon's wax
polish, which was quite different to the polish found in the
McGowan's home'.

When George Clarke, the newsagent, revealed that the paper
which Taylor collected every day was the (Catholic-Nationalist)
Irish News, the judge stopped writing and peered over his spec-

tacles in mock amazement; there were echoing titters in the
court and Taylor managed a wry grin. A momentary relaxation
for all. But the newsagent was firm in his statement that Robert
had not called for his paper either on Friday or Saturday; it lay
uncollected at the end of each day, he said. Robert's friend Billie Booth was equally emphatic in stating that at no time had he
ever borrowed money from him. In saying this he glanced
coldly at the accused and conceded with minimum enthusiasm
that yes, he had known him for several years and met up with
him in pubs, where they talked about dogs and horses (at which
point the alert might have divined just why the Catholic newspaper was Robert's choice). Less emphatic than hitherto in his
evidence supporting the Crown case was Alexander Morrison,
the publican. When questioned by McCoy, the assistant Crown
counsel, he did not specify that Robert's request for a loan took
place in the morning, an omission whose importance McCoy did
not seem to register at that point, but which would trouble
Curran considerably.

Cross-examination by the defence was light and was shared
by Fox and Hanna. Fox put it to Clarke that it was a practice in
many newsagents for customers to come in and, in the absence
of an assistant, lift their paper and leave a penny on the counter;
wouldn't that explain Taylor's apparent failure to collect his
paper on the days mentioned? This suggestion was a curious
blunder, signifying a lack of co-ordination on the part of the
defence team. It would also underline Robert's penchant for the
instant, unconsidered lie: when pressed by Curran sometime
later in the day, he would insist that not only did he collect his
paper but that he also spoke to Clarke, gave him a threepenny
bit and received two-pence change. Hanna's one question was
put to Dr Girvan, the prison's assistant medical officer. He ignored the doctor's observation that he saw scratches on Robert's
face when he was admitted, and instead asked a question which

prepared the way for what he had by now decided would be a key theme in the defence: 'Is he a perfectly normal man?' Not everyone in the jury would have noticed the discrimination in Girvan's reply: 'He *behaved* quite normally.'

Fox opened the case for the defence. His opening words were unctuous and made a general point which was strangely inappropriate to this particular case, even if it gave the impression that the defence's one and only concern was to see that justice was done and not simply to get their client off the hook. 'Gentlemen of the jury,' he said:

> I would ask you to rid your minds of all prejudice which may have arisen as a result of publicity given to the case. Prejudice is the enemy of justice, and to prejudge the case is to attack the very principle of justice. You must make a strong conscious effort to combat the unconscious prejudice which might seep into your minds.

One would have thought that if prejudice were to operate in this case, it was more likely to work in Taylor's favour than the reverse. But perhaps he was uncertain as to whether the screening process which the jury panel had undergone was completely effective. Or perhaps what really prompted his grand admonition was a feeling that any reasonably intelligent jury would already have concluded in the light of the evidence that only one judgment was possible, and that they would take a lot of persuading to change their minds: prejudiced.

Quite rightly, however, he went on to point out that the issue was not whether Taylor was guilty or not but whether or not the Crown had proved him guilty. And the Crown, he contended, had failed to do so. He claimed to find three flaws in the prosecution case. Following the path laid down by Hanna, he first sought to turn the horrific nature of the crime to Taylor's advantage by means of the 'normality' theme. 'The attack on Mrs McGowan was indeed a most brutal, dastardly, sadistic attack,' he said. 'It was not an attack that could have been made by a sane, sober and normal person.' But the Crown had not produced one iota of evidence to suggest that Robert Taylor was an unstable man. He simply did not have the 'mental attitude' required for such an assault. Fox's display of righteous horror was effective; it distanced both himself and the nice-looking, normal young man from the ghastly crime.

Secondly, there was the alleged motive for the murder, a desperate need for money. Taylor, he asserted flatly, had no such need; if he had, 'why did he not take the handbag in McGowan's which contained the money?' It may be stretching interpretation too far to suggest that the phrasing here implies the speaker's assumption that Taylor *was* there and could have taken the handbag. But read as intended, the argument was so feeble that the prosecution did not feel the need to rebut it by stating the obvious (Taylor would not have been looking for coins; and there might have been notes in the bag which he did take – one could not say that he did not steal from it.)

Having intimated that Robert was a perfectly normal and sane person, Fox, again following Hanna, did the reverse for Mrs McGowan. Her statements, he said, if in any way mistaken would put the whole Crown case in jeopardy. And they must have been mistaken. In the first place, the assault could not have lasted more than nine minutes, so she could not have had a good look at her assailant. Moreover, 'in complete and utter contradiction of her religious training she did not ask to see a priest. That was because her mentality had been affected by the assault.' Indeed it had been so affected that she must have been spurred by feelings of anger and revenge to name Robert as the assailant.

Then there was the question of scientific evidence. Taylor's fingerprints were not found in the house, he pointed out; and if the prosecution alleged that he wore gloves, they could not prove it: where were these gloves? Prudently ignoring the presence of barley and blood-stained white hairs on Taylor (less visible to the assailant than his accusing gloves), Fox addressed the problem of blood and produced a surprise which brought his speech to an emphatic conclusion, leaving the way open for Robert to come forth and make everyone think again. If the defence, he said, could establish in a satisfactory manner how the blood got on Taylor's clothes, then the jury should acquit him. And the defence would do just that. Robert was ready now to take the stand and make a claim so preposterous that it would be laughable if the context were not so distressing.

Leaving the prosecution lawyers looking decidedly uneasy and the public suddenly tense with anticipation, Fox resumed his seat at the bench with a swish. Then, at the Clerk of the Court's request, Robert rose from the dock to take his place on the stand. Hanna waited for him with the encouraging flicker of a smile. 'He gave his evidence in a clear and confident manner,' observed the *Irish News*. It was his natural style, but Hanna had rehearsed their question-and-answer session so as to facilitate it; however much they intensified his dislike of the young man, his visits with Anthony Lunn to the grey consulting room in the Gaol had not been wasted. Robert responded almost enthusiastically here to his questions and with answers of great precision and seeming candour. He was, he said, twenty-one years of age and until February this year had been employed by a Mr Barrett of Sunnyside Street. Prior to April he had become engaged to 'a young lady named Elizabeth Jones.' On the morning of 16 April he left his home at 9.45 am and went to Clarke's in York Street to get his copy of *The Irish News* (some more titters from the gallery here). Then he went to the City Hall 'to see Billie Booth about money'. After the afternoon visit from the police he went with his sister-in-law to Morrison's to ask the loan of £20. And so on . . . until on emerging from Houston and Williamson he was approached by Head Constable Thornton and Sergeant Hughes and taken to Glenravel Street.

This smooth narrative, its elements familiar except for the *afternoon* timing of the visit to Morrison and the pleasingly in-offensive 'about money' (Billie no longer a debtor), was really a kind of sedative preamble designed to promote suspension of disbelief for the tall story which was to follow. Hanna intro-duced this ever so gently: 'On your coat and other garments traces of blood were found. Would you tell the Judge and Jury how that blood got on them?' Puzzled (like everyone else), the judge paused once more in his writing; and as if the thoughts of the entire court room were focused in his gaze, he looked down intently at Robert. Almost triumphantly, Robert replied:

'They got on it through my nose bleeding on Good Friday and the Monday before.'

'Where were you when your nose began to bleed?'

'I was lying on the seat in the kitchen.'

'What clothes had you on?'

'I had my top coat over me.'

'Where were you on Monday night when your nose bled?' This question was constructed to address the tricky problem of blood on his socks.

'I was in the lavatory.'

Whether independently or as a result of Hanna's prompting in the grey room, Robert had realised that this narrative required mention of a handkerchief (an obligatory item of dress in the pre-Kleenex era). Conveniently for Robert, the police had found two handkerchiefs, one in his overcoat and one in his trouser pocket, one of them with bloodstains. 'You always carry two handkerchiefs?' asked Hanna. 'Yes,' he replied. 'I always carry an extra one in case my nose begins to bleed.' Evidence against him became evidence for.

A great buzz filled the court room as suspense subsided and people turned to whisper to one another. But Hanna's semblance of a rescue operation was not yet complete. Waiting until all was still again, he ended with a question-and-answer routine whose insistent monosyllables suggested truth pared down to its indestructible essentials:

'Did you know Mrs McGowan?'

'Yes.'

'Had you worked for her?'

'Yes.'

'Did you see her on the 16th April?'

'No.'

'Did you make any attack on her?'

'No.'

'That day or any other day?'

'No.'

'Did you attempt to throttle her?'

'No.'

'Did you kick her?'

'No.'

'Did you go into her house on that day?'

'No.'

That the third question made the next five questions redundant is a logical nicety that would have been missed by most listeners in the clamorous rhetoric of denial which followed. After the sixth 'no', Hanna breathed heavily and sat down. His junior counsel turned to him with a look of affectionate admiration.

The Attorney General now approached Robert; and if the young man was nervous he did not show it. But Curran immediately raised the question of money and motive, and in so doing did much to dispel the illusion of truth and candour. He got Robert to agree that he had been unemployed for two months before 16 April, and that he had at most on that day the sum of

£5 when in fact he needed £12.9s for the taxi firm and another three or four pounds for a ring. He also got him to agree that he had lied to both the police and Houston and Williamson in saying that Booth owed him money. But Curran would not let Robert rest with that admission. He asked him *why* he lied to the police about Booth, and Robert's answer fully explains why he would locate his visit to Morrison in the afternoon and enlist Erkine to confirm the timing:

'I didn't want the police to know I was borrowing money when they were seeing me.'

'Why?'

'Well, they were around seeing me about an assault that had been committed.'

'I say again, why?'

'Well, it would look bad for me at that time.'

'Is it because it would give you reason for assaulting Mrs McGowan?'

'Yes.'

'So when the police came to you it occurred to you that the fact that you had tried to borrow money that morning would be against you?'

'Yes.'

'It might lead the police to believe that you had assaulted Mrs McGowan?'

'Yes.'

The series of guilty-sounding yeses wrung from Robert echoed and undid the strenuous noes produced by Hanna. But Curran had more to do before the pretence of truth was fully exposed as sham. Since he still stuck to his claim that he had bought *The Irish News* ('I put a threepenny bit on the counter and Mr Clarke gave me my paper'), Curran compelled him to acknowledge that Clarke said otherwise. And concerning Mrs Shiels's statement that she saw him at midday (she who knew him well by sight, having employed him on two occasions), he was driven to say: 'That cannot be true.' The unlikely possibility that both of these witnesses were lying or mistaken could not be missed.

Then Curran approached the big question of blood and bleeding, his strategy here being to get Robert to confess that he had lied about blood originally, so that it would seem there was no more cause to assume he was telling the truth now than he had been hitherto. In the face of relentless questioning, Robert soon became entangled in evasion and self-contradiction. Hanna and Fox watched grimly from the Bench, his father looked tense and white-faced in his seat nearby:

'Why did you tell the police that the stains on your clothes were caused by paint?'

'Well, it could have been paint . . . I thought it was paint.'

'Why?'

'Because I work with paint.'

'Did it occur to you that having bloodstains on your coat would be against you in connection with the assault on Mrs McGowan?'

'I didn't think about it. The police said they were bloodstains. I didn't know it was blood.'

'Did you remember at that time that your nose had been bleeding the day before?'

'I never thought about it.'

'Has your nose bled since?'

'No. It's only when I am painting that it bleeds.'

'Have you had medical attention at any time for your nose?'

'No.'

'Can you explain how the blood got on the shoulder of your overcoat?'

'No.'

'All this nose-bleeding happened the day before?'

'Yes.'

'And did it not occur to you to tell the truth about it?'

'No.'

'Did you know the blood on your coat and trousers was blood?'

'I suppose I did.'

This was bad, but the situation became much worse when Curran asked about the bloodstained sock and hairs, and the judge joined in the questioning:

'Just explain how that splash of blood could have got down to your foot from your nose bleeding.'

'It could have dropped down when I was in the lavatory.'

'Did you notice any splash on your right leg?'

'I knew it was dropping down.'

'If you knew that why then did you not tell the police that the stain on your sock and foot was caused by your nose bleeding?'

'I did not think of that.'

'I see. Now how do you account for the fact that the blood-stained hairs on your coat match those on Mrs McGowan's head?'

[After a long pause] 'I don't know.'

At this point the judge intervened and repeated the last question and again Taylor said, 'I don't know.' Curran then put his final question: 'How do you account for the fact that one of the bloodstains on your coat was still wet?' To which Robert replied: 'I don't know how it was wet.'

Curran turned his back on him as if in contempt and invited Hanna to bring on his next witness. Looking wretched, Robert made his way back to the dock, dismissed from the posture of truth and assurance in which Hanna had left him. His usual, up-right stance, the small man using every inch of his height, deserted him en route.

The last defence witness of the day responded promptly to the clerk's call. Stout, rose-cheeked and motherly, Mrs Mary Walker from Tiger's Bay puffed her way up to the stand. She may have looked ordinary, but in the view of some lawyers and one judge she was the most extraordinary witness they had ever encountered. Indeed there was a hint of procedural irregularity in her contribution to the day's events. The exact route by which she arrived at her present position was never made clear. Did she approach Anthony Lunn and make a sworn statement on Robert's behalf, which he and Hanna realised on reflection they could not use in the manner she intended? And, knowing it would be unlawful to get her to alter the statement in such a way as to effect her intention, did they then decide that her evidence could still be put to good use, though to an end she had not envisaged? And did they rehearse her accordingly?

As she indicated in court, Robert was a friend of her two daughters and she had known him for over three years. She heard on Easter Tuesday that he was accused of murder and that the assault had taken place on Saturday between 12.00 and 12.30. And without mentioning it to the police, even when she visited Robert in prison in company with his parents, she made her way to the defence lawyer and told him she had seen Robert on High Street in the city centre at 12.20 and that she was prepared to swear to that. 'I was on the bus at the time with my daughter,' she said in court to defence counsel Fox. And she authenticated what Curran later called 'this story' with a rush of circumstantial realism. 'He was wearing a heavy blue overcoat, the belt was hanging loose. And he had his hands in his pockets. He was bareheaded and wore a brown suit. I nodded to him with my head and he nodded back. I knew the time was 12.20 because I had just been looking out at the clock over McDowell's the jeweller.'

The trouble with what could have been a beautiful story was that Robert's statement put him at a distance from High Street all morning, and speeding at 12.15 on the Cavehill Road bus that would drop him at Lilliput Street for his alleged encounter with Lily and her sister at 12.30. Defence counsel Fox did not point to this contradiction. He did not seem to be troubled by it; it was as if he *wanted* Walker to be seen as wrong – but honestly wrong; not deceitful, just utterly convinced she was right. He simply asked, 'Have you any doubt in your own mind that the person you saw at that time was Robert?' To which she responded, 'No, I am positive it was Robert Taylor.'

In his severe and sarcastic cross-examination, Curran made much of the fact that she had not gone to the police with this crucial information even though she believed (in his words) that it 'would establish beyond any doubt that Robert Taylor had not committed this assault'. A normal, honest, law-abiding citizen, he implied, would go straight to the police with evidence of that kind. And when she explained that she did not approach the police 'for personal reasons', he pursed his lips and nodded his head knowingly, indicating thus that he would not allude to her recent little problem with the law. Instead, he tied her up in self-contradiction, getting her to say 'I made a mistake' when he pointed out that she had begun by telling him she had not told her daughter she saw Robert and later insisting she had told her. 'You know that Taylor denies what you say?' he asked sternly. Completely unabashed, she responded: 'I still say I saw him. No mistake about it.'

She was unabashed because she knew it had become her role to be proven wrong: to show that a sincere and honest Protestant woman can be mistaken in her evidence just as a sincere and honest Catholic can too. The finger of Hanna was pointing at a key witness of the prosecution, Mrs Shiels, and even at the murdered woman too. Nothing could alter the impression of deep-dyed guilt left by Robert's performance in the stand, nor his gloom as he was led down the bleak tunnel leading from the

Courthouse to the Gaol. But at the day's end Mrs Mary Walker
of Syringa Street had given many observers some cause for
head-scratching amusement – and a teasing suggestion of
lawyerly *legerdemain*. It would not be the last suggestion of its
kind in the attempt to rescue Robert the Painter from the hangman's noose.

16

HIGH ABOVE THE COURTHOUSE the goddess Justice with her
scales looked white and magnificent against a perfect blue
sky on the morning of 28 July. The good weather injected a
touch of the holiday mood into many of those waiting to witness
the conclusion of the trial. As on the morning before, a long
queue, the width of three or four people, stretched down the
steps of the Courthouse and across the forecourt and snaked
well up the road outside. The police were present in strength to
keep order. Even when the doors of the Courthouse were closed
at 10.20 and the front gates locked, people remained in queues
throughout the day in the hope of gaining entrance as others left.
Near the close of the trial, when it was reported that the jury had
retired, the number outside had grown to about five hundred.
They were stretched on either side of the Crumlin Road and police were posted at the gates to prevent them from getting in.
Everyone knew that this was no ordinary murder trial.

It was a long day for all and, for some, agonisingly so, since
the jury was out for over three hours and did not return its verdict until 9.40 pm. As on the previous day, many refused to
come out at lunch time and by the end of the day there were
some inside who had not eaten since morning. The prospect of a
death sentence, with all its terrible solemnity, combined with the
tedium of their own lives and the sectarian subtext of the trial,
served to magnetise the citizens of this drab and divided city.

Thin, pallid and pregnant, Robert's fiancée, Lily Jones, had come strangely dressed: all in black, and with a black veil thrown over her head and face: a clear attempt, surely, to steal some of the sympathy which Kathleen, also in mourning, would have won from everyone present. When she was swearing by Almighty God to tell the truth, the whole truth and nothing but the truth, she broke down and cried. Hanna waited compassionately until she recovered and elicited from her the now familiar alibi: Robert had arrived at her home at 12.25 looking in no way unusual and left five minutes later. When invited, Curran declined to cross-examine her: why add to the pain of a creature whimpering in a steel trap? She had no choice but to commit perjury and, whatever the outcome of the trial, the future for her was dark.

Madeline Connor's part in the agreed fiction was to flesh out and substantiate her brother's tale about nose-bleeding, and this she did without wavering. On Good Friday, she explained, Robert was lying on the settee in their living room in Meadow Street with his coat over him. She noticed there was blood on the back of his hand. He had his hand up to his nose and he said his nose was bleeding. In cross examination, Curran ignored all this; he put only one question, and one she clearly did not anticipate; her response undermined what her father intended to say on the same subject. Showing her the spanner found in McGowan's, he asked her if she could identify it, and she said:

'I saw a few like that knockin' about the house.'

'Of the same shape, colour and size?'

'I think so. Yes.'

This reply fell too nicely into Curran's lap for him to spoil its effect by further questioning. He dismissed her coolly, returned to the bench, and he and his colleagues lay in wait for Robert senior, who came next to the stand. Madeline looked apologetically at her father as she passed him on the way down.

Hanna began his questioning of the father by attempting in his recognisable style to recapture the image of a Robert who bore no resemblance to the one presented by the prosecution:

'Tell us, Mr Taylor, in a few simple words, and speaking as a father, what sort of person is Robert?'

'Robert is a good boy.'

'Have you ever, ever, known him to be violent?'

'No! Never!'

'Now tell us what happened in your home on the morning of the 16th April.'

The father then told a tale of domestic peace and familial normality abruptly broken by the arrival of two policemen who took his son into the sitting room to question him about some assault: 'I was sitting by the fireside when my son came in about 12.45 or one o'clock, nothing unusual about his appearance . . ..' His tone of voice did not imply resentment at this treatment; it suggested rather the long-suffering patience of the working class, a humble, law-abiding family cooperating with the police in their inquiries.

He was cross-examined by Jones, KC, the third prosecution counsel. The questions focused on the two items of evidence with which he should have had most acquaintance, the spanner and the nosebleeding. Perhaps he was unnerved by Madeline's concession, for Jones soon had him entangled in his own answers. When shown the spanner found in Mrs McGowan's and asked if it came from his house, he replied: 'I couldn't say.' Later however he said that all the spanners in his house were rusty and handmade by his friends in the shipyard – both of which facts clearly implied that the spanner on display did not come from his house. Then he was asked if it was not true that his son-in-law had brought some tools back from the RAF in 1945 and that the one marked 'F33 . . . forged in the USA' was one of them. He paused and then said that Head Constable Thornton 'took that spanner from the house' when he came to question Robert: in other words, it was not the spanner used in the assault. He may have gambled here that the Head Constable was not in court that day, but Thornton was sitting at the back of the hall and was asked by Jones and the judge to come forward. He said: 'I took no spanner out of his house. I brought it down to his house.' Turning aside from his note-taking, Judge Sheil looked down at the witness and shook his head in a silent 'tut, tut!'

Asked about Robert's alleged affliction, the father seemed to recover from his discomfiture and spoke at first with impressive vividness. The bleeding happened about twice a week. He often tried to get the lad to see a doctor about it but he always refused. When he slept with him he often woke in the morning with his shirt 'soaked in blood and . . . had to change into another shirt'. The nose bleeding occurred also when he was painting; and it would last from twenty to thirty minutes. Jones did not ask why neither Robert's employer, nor one of his workmates, nor a customer had been brought forward to give evidence in support of this extraordinary claim. But he did ask how it was that blood got on to Robert's jacket, overcoat and socks while his overalls showed not a single trace of blood. The father was flummoxed once more. Jones kept putting this question in different ways and every response was helpless:

'I couldn't tell you.'

'I just can't say.'

'I couldn't tell you.'

'I didn't take any particular notice.'

Lily's sister, Mrs Mary Erskine, the last witness for the defence, was cross-questioned by Curran. She told how she was at home from work when Robert arrived at 12.25 ('nothin' peculiar about him'), and how she went round to his house about 1.45, having been frightened by the visit of the police. Robert asked her, she said, to go with him down to Morrison's. She stood outside the pub at the side door when he went in. After-wards they phoned Houston and Williamson and made the arrangement. Curran was unable to weaken the 12.25 alibi she gave Robert, but he did expose a weakness in the claim designed to shift his visit to Morrison from the morning to the afternoon.

'Why did you have to go with Robert to Morrison's?'

'Because he asked me.'

'But for what purpose?'

'None at all.'

'Why didn't Lily go with him? Was it usual for you to be going out with him on such occasions?'

'I would go out with him sometimes, like when he was lookin' for cigarettes.'

'For what purpose did you go with Robert to Morrison's?'

'None at all.'

Curran smiled ironically, paused and then asked with mock politeness, 'I suggest you were not there?' To which she responded, petulantly: 'I was.'

Awkwardness and implausibility hung in the air; but since Morrison was now leaning in Robert's direction, failing to specify a morning visit, there was nothing Curran could do to further weaken Erskine's evidence. Morrison, who had become as much a defence witness as a Crown witness, was a source of considerable irritation to him, yet he knew enough about life for a publican on York Street and at the edge of Tiger's Bay not to judge him too harshly.

Between 1939 and the Troubles of 1970, the province had been relatively free of sectarian strife. That was partly because of the war and its aftermath but partly too because the riots of summer 1935 were vividly remembered, especially by Catholics, who were the chief victims of the violence: 'The great majority of the wounded were Catholic; over two thousand

Catholics and only a handful of Protestants were driven from
their homes; and ninety-five per cent of the £21,669 compensa-
tion for destruction of property was paid to Catholics' (Jonathan
Bardon, *A History of Ulster*, second edition, Blackstaff Press,
2001, p. 541). The storm centre of the violence was the York
Street area, and a publican such as Morrison would not have
needed reminding by Robert Taylor's friends and sympathisers
that pubs and publicans on and around York Street had been
favourite targets. He would surely have remembered that among
the murdered publicans was a young bachelor called McKiernan, shot dead in his tiny back-street pub in front of a few terrified customers by two gunmen who defiantly looked them in the
face before pocketting their revolvers and walking out. Renowned in the Gaelic Athletic Association as a champion high
jumper, McKiernan had come up as an apprentice barman from
County Tyrone; after the funeral his mother sold out for a song.
But Morrison might not have remembered that at the trial of the
two men accused of murdering McKiernan, Attorney General
A.B. Babington (Unionist MP and a staunch Orangeman) had
said: 'The man was a publican and a Roman Catholic and therefore liable to assassination.' The accused, both Orangemen,
were acquitted. An enormous crowd outside the Courthouse
sang 'God save the King' and bonfires were lit all along York
Street to celebrate their release.

17

ONE HOUR EACH WAS ALLOTTED by the judge to the contending counsels to present their address to the jury: the
balance of justice. In fact, Hanna took one hour and forty-three
minutes, Curran (after lunch) slightly less than an hour. Hanna
seemed to sense that repetitive and varied expression of the
same idea was necessary if his claims were to seem plausible,

whereas Curran clearly believed his arguments needed no elabo-
ration, the truth of the case being evident by now to any body of
sensible men. But this difference of style dictated by circum-
stance was due also to a temperamental difference: Hanna was
an expansive, theatrical speaker, Curran crisp and dry. The
judge's charge, summarising and evaluating all the evidence and
arguments with as much impartiality as possible, took an ex-
hausting three hours. And then at 6.33 pm the twelve-man jury
was sent off to consider its verdict.

Hanna began by implying his sympathetic oneness with the
jury and trying to win them emotionally to his side while denying that he was doing so. The purpose of this strategy was not
only to counter any suspicion that his arguments were insensitive but ultimately to make his client's nature seem remote from
the inhumanity of the crime for which he stood accused.

There had, he said, been a horrible and brutal murder committed after an assault at the house of the deceased. So in the
circumstances it was impossible for all – himself and his client
no less that the jury – not to feel an acute sense of strain. Still,
he was not appealing to the jury for sympathy. No, for this was a
case in which they could with complete confidence acquit the
young prisoner.

He had to remind them that the charge of murder against
Robert Taylor was based entirely on Mary McGowan's evidence. But, with respect, what else was that but evidence from
the grave? What would her evidence be if she were here now
and cross-examined on oath? Would she be unshaken and un-
shakeable in her claim that it was Robert who attacked her? She
would almost certainly seem to the jury to be perfectly sincere,
being a devout, religious woman and a good neighbour. But
they had all seen by now that a sincere witness can also be a
very faulty one. Sincerity was a noble virtue, but in a court of

law, and where a young man's life was at stake, it was not enough. Truth, however, painful, was what they sought.

Now the painful truth one had to face was this: that Mrs McGowan was dealt several heavy blows, one near the portion of the brain which controls the higher intellect, namely reason and memory. Thus her subsequent account of what happened was necessarily defective; she could not have thought clearly and distinctly or remembered clearly and distinctly. Moreover, one had to bear in mind the fact that her back was turned to the man who tried to strangle her and that the whole dreadful affair was over in nine or ten minutes, a storm of violence that left no clear trace in her mind of what had happened or who was involved.

Lest this argument might not work, Hanna recalled what he had emphasised earlier, namely that Mrs McGowan, who wore bifocals, would probably have failed to see her assailant clearly in the confined space of the narrow hallway, just as Mrs Shiels, who also wore spectacles, mistook for Robert someone whom she saw passing on the other side of Atlantic Avenue.

As to why Mary McGowan should have named Robert as her assailant rather than anyone else, one had to remember that wild accusation was a feature of distressed and disordered minds and that it could be motivated by obscure resentment, irrational anger, vindictiveness. Recall, he said, that the deceased was critical of Robert's work and that he asked to be taken off his last job for her. *De mortuis nil nisi bonum*, 'Say nothing but good about the dead', was an admirable maxim of the ancient Romans. He concurred with it wholeheartedly and did not wish to sully in the slightest the good name of the dead woman. But the Mary McGowan he spoke of now was not herself, she was irreparably damaged, changed. As any one of us would have been in the circumstances. The circumstances were such as, at the very least, to cast reasonable doubt on the value of her evidence.

Then there was the question of bloodstains on Taylor's clothing. They had been adequately accounted for by his history of nosebleeding. It was unfortunate that he failed to mention this when first questioned by the police, but he was a young man placed in an extremely stressful situation and it was natural enough that he should fail to mention a physical problem which he took for granted and hardly gave a thought to.

The prosecution had made much of the question of motive. But, he asked them, was it at all plausible that Robert Taylor would have committed this murder? On reflection, any sensible person would surely say 'no'. The prosecution had alleged that money was his motive. But there was no evidence that any money could have been found in that house: they had heard only of some silver and coppers in a handbag, a trifling sum. They had to bear in mind too that there were valuables in the house which had not been taken; if theft had been the motive, they surely would have been taken. They had heard much about the £12.9s which Taylor needed; but was it not preposterous to suggest that he or any sane person would be prepared to commit murder for such a sum?

Any sane person. That, he said, brought him to the nub of the argument. Everyone in that courtroom agreed that the assault committed on this poor lady was cruel and barbarous in the extreme. Emphatically, it was not the act of a normal human being but of someone completely deranged. Now they had it on the best medical evidence that Robert Taylor was a perfectly normal young man, with, as his father reminded them, a record free from all suggestion of violence: 'a good boy'. Concluding, he said he had every confidence that the jury would have reasonable doubt as to Robert Taylor's guilt. That being so, they were duty bound to acquit him.

Mary McGowan's evidence was uppermost in the Attorney General's thoughts when he addressed the jury after the lunch break. He emphasised that as soon as she staggered out of the rear of her house into the friendly arms of Mrs Rafferty, she stated who committed the assault. And that was not a single statement nor one unheard by any but Mrs Rafferty. Mr Skillen heard it. It was repeated on two separate occasions to Sergeant Davis and also to Doctor Lynch.

If the jury believed Mrs McGowan's statements, statements made when she believed she was dying as a result of this violence, then the case required no further evidence. And why should they not accept Mrs McGowan's evidence? The prosecution had alleged that her understanding was gravely impaired by the blows to the head she had received and that in consequence she would not have identified her assailant correctly. But when she opened the door and let him in to use the phone, she did so precisely because she knew him. Moreover, the concern she showed for the effect which her terrible condition would have on her husband and daughter, and the practical steps she asked to be taken, indicate very clearly that, despite her intense suffering, her mind was unaffected.

And why else should she name 'Robert the painter' as her assailant if it were not true? The imputation to her of a revenge motive was deeply regrettable and wholly without foundation or plausibility. There was not the slightest suggestion that Taylor had ever done her an injury. A revenge motive was not something which deserved a moment's attention. It simply did not fit the character of this good woman, a woman who believed she would soon be facing her Maker.

Mary McGowan's evidence would have been sufficient in itself to establish Taylor's guilt, but it was given a solid foundation by evidence of a different nature. Taylor was shown to have lied to the police in order to distance himself from the scene of the crime. Nothing had been done by the defence to negate the significance of the fact that shoe polish of a kind used by the

Taylor family had been found on the soles of the victim's shoes; that cereal of the kind used by her in the soup she was preparing, together with fibres matching those from her carpet, were found on Taylor's shoes; that white hairs microscopically identical to hers were found on his coat. And then, of course, there were the bloodstains on his overcoat, jacket, trousers, shoe, socks and foot. They were the marks of a violent assault. When questioned by the police on the day of the assault, Taylor said they were paint stains for the simple reason that he knew they would incriminate him. But now he tells us that they were caused by nosebleeding and that he was afflicted with this problem twice a week for several years. It simply defied belief that when asked by the police to account for the numerous stains on his clothing he would have forgotten this alleged malady or forgotten the alleged fact that he had had a serious nosebleed the day before.

As he had explained at the outset of the trial, the Crown was not obliged to produce a motive for the crime, but motive there clearly was. He did not wish to dwell on Taylor's special responsibility to poor Miss Jones. Suffice it to say that he was committed to marry her on Easter Monday and that on Saturday morning he was at his wits' end to get the money to cover the wedding expenses. Armed with a spanner, seven feet of strong cord and a pair of gloves, he made his way to the home of this unfortunate woman and committed a most brutal and premeditated murder.

The Crown, he concluded, had by their cross-examination of the defence witnesses made the case against the accused even stronger than it had been at the outset. They had presented established facts which led to one conclusion only – the conviction of Taylor. Whatever the jury might feel about the consequences of their verdict (clearly he was thinking here of the death sentence) they must all, he said, face the facts and their consequences and say that Robert Taylor murdered Mary McGowan.

Relatively little of what Judge Sheil said in his three-hour summation has survived. The official transcript of the trial housed in the Northern Ireland Records Office stops before all the defence witnesses have been questioned (perhaps because the scheduled retrial made completion unnecessary). Two septuagenerians who attended the trial remember only that for them the effect of the judge's charge was obliterated by what happened when the jury eventually returned. *The Irish News*, the paper which reported the trial most extensively, gave only a short two-paragraph summary of the summing up. This was due partly to the fact that the judge exhaustively recapitulated what had already been said; but sheer fatigue and insufficient time must have been reasons too. The reporter would have got back to his office in Donegall Street somewhere around 10.30 pm (since the jury did not return until 9.40) and then he and his assistant had to work through the night to get the report ready for the morning edition. By the time he reached the judge's three-hour marathon in his report, extreme brevity was inevitable. What his report gave prominence to, but without comment, was the nuancing in the judge's parting advice to the jury: '[I]f they were satisfied beyond a reasonable doubt of the prisoner's guilt, a verdict rendered because of fear of the consequences would violate the oath which each of them had taken.' The judge had tipped the scales in the direction of the Crown: gently, since force was unnecessary.

The Unionist *News-Letter* by contrast chose to end its brief summary of the judge's charge by picking out a sentence from his *opening* remarks (reported as such in *The Belfast Telegraph*) that seemed to tip the balance in Taylor's favour: the jury 'should not allow themselves to be carried away by natural feelings of horror at such a foul and brutal murder and strike at the

first person charged with the crime' – which made readers think
of Hanna's innocent youth.

The judge looked drained when he withdrew from the court
room, courteously ushering the senior barristers before him.
Head Constable Thornton, who had escorted Kathleen
McGowan to and from the Courthouse each day, brought her out
to the entrance hall and found her a seat and a cup of tea; he had
taken her father's place, 'a kind man', she says. At the far end of
the foyer, Kathleen caught sight of Lily, her sister Mary and
Robert's parents; she felt deeply confused in her feelings towards them, alien and yet akin. Lily's parents, however, were
not seen. They had made themselves invisible and inaudible
since the police first knocked on their door, as if trying to avoid
all the shame and notoriety their daughter's connection with
Taylor had incurred.

In the court room and at the press table it was assumed that
the jury would return within an hour – a decent interval. After an
hour and a half hunger and impatience turned restless feet and
incessant chatter into a babble of noise. Mrs Gibbons and her
friend Mrs Sharkey were determined, having got this far, to stay
to the end. Young Gerald Dowd, dodging his summer job at the
Somerton Arms, and disappointed that he had not been called as
a witness (having identified the bottle used in the assault), had
made a special effort to attend the last day of the trial; but he was
overcome by hunger and left at eight o'clock: not good enough,
he would later say, for a future lawyer. By nine o'clock, people
were desperately trying to imagine the scene in the jury room
and the reasons for the delay. Was the jury split down the middle, locked in an evenly balanced contest? Or were one or two
individuals holding out against the majority and frustrating the
unanimous verdict without which a sentence was impossible?
Was there someone there for whom the thought of hanging, the
merciless finality of capital punishment, blocked out all other

considerations? Were they all too tired and confused to think and argue as clearly as was required? Was the foreman trying manfully to persuade the dissident few to join the majority and accept a guilty verdict? (Mrs Gibbons, who said she recognised him, did not think so.)

When at 9.40 the Clerk of the Crown and Peace emerged and faced the crowd, the effect was magical: even before he spoke, people sat down, silence was instantaneous. The judge and the lawyers resumed their places; led by their foreman, the jury filed awkwardly and self-consciously into their box, having been out for over three hours. Taylor was led to the dock, where he stood erect, facing the judge, gripping the rails tightly. When the jury had settled, the clerk nodded to the foreman, who arose and came forward to present him with a piece of paper. Taylor, wrote the ever-observant *Irish News* man, paled and kept biting his lip nervously as the Jury's decision was being handed to the Clerk. In a moment of great tension, Mr Pollock raised the paper and said: 'Gentlemen, you have not arrived at a decision.' Taylor, on hearing this, gave a deep sigh of relief that was quite audible at the press table. He moistened his lips with his tongue and relaxed the rigid position in which he was standing.

Judge Sheil said that he had no doubt that the jury had done their utmost to arrive at an agreement. He granted Crown Counsel's request to have the prisoner put back in custody for trial at the next Belfast City Commission on 18 October. Taylor was then taken below. 'There was a remarkable scene when the news of the Jury's decision reached the crowd outside,' said *The Irish News*. 'A section of them began to cheer and some rushed to pat the prisoner's father and fiancée on the back as they were proceeding from the Courthouse to the Gaol to see Taylor.'

*

Some friends of Mrs Gibbons who had not attended the trial were taken aback by the calmness with which she reported the jury's failure to return a verdict. Given the fact that the prosecution seemed to have presented a watertight case against Taylor, and given too her husband's friendship with Mr McGowan, they expected her to express astonishment and outrage. The laconic explanation she gave for her calmness seems now to reach beyond herself and the trials of Robert the Painter to encompass a deep-rooted cynicism in the attitude of the Nationalist community towards the organs of the Ulster Establishment: 'With Mr McKenzie as foreman of the jury, what else would you expect?'

But she and her family and friends were only half right in the conclusion they drew from this. It was not, as they thought, the case of an authoritative and prejudiced personality exercising undue influence on a number of his colleagues, since – unknown to anyone in Newington at the time, and thanks to the archives of the Northern Ireland Records Office – it can now be revealed that only one member of the jury rejected a guilty verdict.

18

THE RETRIAL BEGAN ON MONDAY 24 October and lasted five days. For the superstitious, the weather was ominous. Great gusts of wind blew sullen clouds across the skies when on Monday morning, from as early as 6.30, people began to collect outside the Courthouse for the 10.30 opening. No more easy chat in the morning sun, but hunched shoulders, raincoats and rebellious umbrellas. By Tuesday morning and until Friday violent storms swept across the whole of Ireland and Britain; trees and buildings were blown down; the *Queen Elizabeth* berthed one day late after its roughest crossing ever. Inside the court, however, the Clerk of the Crown and Peace and the Under-Sheriff calmly supervised an ordered ritual designed to advance towards a just conclusion in accord with ancient rules unaffected by environmental phenomena.

This sense of order within was enhanced by a double repetition: not only the ritual but its content was the same as before. There was a new judge, Sir James Andrews KC, but this was less change than an enhancement in the seriousness and dignity of the proceedings, for Andrews was the Lord Chief Justice. The prosecution and defence teams were the same, and there were the same witnesses telling the same stories. But the new trial was not for the lawyers a tiresome re-run of what went before; it was like a contest between runners who had tied at the finish of the first race and now had to strain more than ever to win the second. For the uninvolved spectators who had attended the first trial, and for those of them who had not done so but had come equipped with what the newspapers had told them in July, the experience had the pleasure of re-reading a thriller with possibly new clues, plot twists and a different ending. But for the Taylor family, it was more anguish, no less pure than before; by the end of this trial, sixty-four-year-old Robert senior had become an old man, with not long to live.

It was more pain too for Kathleen McGowan. In his address to the jury on the last day of the trial, the judge would pause gallantly before considering the evidence to say that 'the most tragic figure in the whole case was Elizabeth Jones, who, but for this tragedy, would have been a married woman today. One could not help feeling sorry for her . . . as she struggled to keep back the tears in the box.' Lily's tears had more effect on the judge's manly heart than Kathleen McGowan's restrained demeanour, her mourning attire (Hanna's masterstroke?) more than the bereaved daughter's. Again, no one acknowledged what Kathleen had to endure in this re-enactment: 'Do you recognise that person? Have you seen this bent knife before? This pot? This spanner? Do you recognise this dress? Do these photographs show the body of your mother?' And then she had to listen to those graphic recitals of what was seen and heard in her home on Easter Saturday morning. By the end of the trial, she was a young woman with but one desire. To flee.

For most of those who attended the second trial, its most enduring impression was probably shaped by the arguments centring on Robert's stained clothing: spilt blood, the archetypal symbol of guilt's indelible mark. Both the defence and the prosecution had come prepared to reinforce their arguments on this issue. Robert had decided it would be helpful if he could offer some plausible and precise explanation for his chronic nosebleeds; he also realised that if he hadn't had a single nose-bleed during his six months in gaol, the reality of this alleged weakness might seem questionable. So he said that bleeding was caused specifically by the smell of gloss paint and claimed that he had had two nose-bleeds in gaol, one on 12 September and the other on the night of 6 October. He had not been painting himself, nor had anyone else, but the corridors in his wing of the prison had been freshly tarred and the smell of that, he alleged, had affected him. Hanna produced two witnesses to support this claim: Robert McAuley, a hospital attendant at the prison, and Hugh Girvan, the prison doctor. Neither they nor anyone else had actually seen Robert's nose bleeding, but he said that it occurred during the night and showed them blood on his pillow and sheet. Questioned by Hanna, these two witnesses proved to be less than enthusiastic supporters of Robert's story; yet if the lawyer was disgruntled, he concealed the fact with a characteristic show of airy satisfaction.

Regarding the first nose-bleed, McAuley said that he had asked Robert why he had waited two days to report it; to which Robert, instinctively performing the innocent-boy act assigned to him by Hanna, had answered, 'I didn't think it was of any importance.' On both occasions Dr Girvan was called in to examine him. On the first occasion he had found that Robert had varicose veins in both nostrils but could not find any evidence of bleeding in nostrils, ears or throat. Blatantly disregarding the doctor's scepticism, Hanna asked with reference to 12 September: 'Was that the only occasion on which *there has been nose-bleeding*?' The doctor refused to cooperate, replying: 'There was another *alleged* attack on the night of 6 October', but on the following morning, when summoned by the warder, he could find 'no evidence of any fresh or clotted blood. His mouth, throat, ears etc. were quite normal.' With impressive insouciance, Hanna persisted in referring to these alleged nose-bleeds as medically established facts: in the course of his questioning on the following day, he said to Robert: 'You have heard from Dr Girvan that your nose bled recently while in prison.' Presumably he was telling the jury that they had heard the same.

The prosecution's addition to its case in this matter came from Dr Firth, the forensic scientist brought over from England. He had been asked to consider the likelihood of a nosebleed causing the numerous bloodstains which he had identified on Robert's clothing. He now said that the thick stain on the accused's socks and ankle was simply not consistent with nose-bleeding, even as Robert explained it; if he had been sitting on the toilet when his nose bled, his trousers would have covered his lower leg and ankles. Furthermore, the possibility of blood falling from his nose on to five out of six coat buttons on the overcoat and completely missing the surrounding fabric – while the coat covered the horizontal figure of its owner – was 'extremely remote' (an understatement indeed).

Cross-examining Robert, Curran began by focusing attention on the claim that gloss paint caused his nose to bleed. He proceeded with dry and nagging scepticism, disproving nothing but making improbability speak for itself.

'How long did it take you in your profession as a painter to discover that gloss paint caused your nose to bleed?'

'About two months.'

'Your nose might bleed two or three times a week because of the smell of gloss paint?'

'Well, yes.'

'Did it not occur to you that this was not a suitable occupation?'

'No.'

'Did you ever suggest to anyone before that it was the smell of gloss paint that caused your nose to bleed?'

'Oh yes.'

'Did you ever suggest it in court?'

'I suggest it today.'

'But until today did you ever suggest it?'

'No.'

'Why did you not think of that before?'

'I wasn't asked.'

Knowing that these last questions would be taken as alluding to the first as well as the second trial, Curran permitted himself one of his rare, saturnine smiles, followed by a few moments of thoughtful silence. And then: 'I see.' This was more effective than verbalised logic.

The almost impertinent coolness with which Robert answered here began to elude him when Curran addressed the improbability of his answers at Glenravel Street about blood and paint; he struggled on the edge of self-contradiction (denying and in effect admitting the same thing) and sounded like a man who for some time had been longing to be somewhere, anywhere else.

'When your attention was drawn to the bloodstains on your coat and the police asked you to account for it, you said it was paint?'

'Yes.'

'Why did you tell a lie?'

'I never thought of my nose bleeding.'

'Why didn't you tell them about your nose?'

'I was thinking more of getting out of the barracks.'

'Were you afraid that if you admitted it was blood, it would be evidence against you?'

'But I thought it wasn't blood.'

'Wasn't the statement about it being paint a deliberate lie?'

'Yes.'

'You knew it was not paint?'

'Well, it was a brownish colour.'

'Were you asked by the police how the blood got on your foot?'

'Yes, but I never answered them.'

'Why?'

'I was fed up that night.'

'You didn't suggest that the blood came from your nose?'

'No.'

'Why not?'

['Angrily', says the *Irish News*] 'I told you. I was fed up that night.'

Then there was the difficult practical question as to how the blood got from his nose to the shoulder and buttons of his overcoat when he was allegedly lying on the settee on the night before the assault. For the second trial he sought to improve the plausibility of this story by saying that he had been painting two rooms in the house prior to the nose-bleed; but this did little to blunt the effectiveness of Curran's cross-examination; if anything, it sharpened it. Curran led his victim gently into the next trap, asking him why he lay on the settee that night ('I was tired'), if there was a fire in the kitchen ('Yes') and if the kitchen was cosy ('Pretty cosy').

'If you were cosy, as you say you were, what was the necessity to have your overcoat over you?'

'To keep out the draught.'

'Was there a smell of paint in the house?'

'Yes.'

'Where was it coming from?'

'From the front room.'

'You didn't think of closing the kitchen door, although there was a draught?'

'I was just lying down. I wasn't worrying about my nose!'

'Did you not think your nose would bleed?'

'No.'

'Although there was a smell of paint?'

['Prisoner made no answer.' – *Irish News.*]

Curran then put it to him that if the blood got on to his over-coat it must also have got on to his pullover and the cushion. And Robert felt obliged to say that it did. 'Were these shown to the police?' asked Curran; and the answer was 'No'. There was no need to ask, 'Why not?'

In describing and demonstrating how the blood got on to his overcoat (produced in court for this demonstration) Robert twice contradicted himself, saying first that he lay on his left side and later that he lay on his right side; first that he got off the settee to fetch his handkerchief and later that he reached into his pocket for it. Curran drew his attention to each contradiction and then sternly asked why he gave different answers to the same questions. The replies came back weakly, pathetically; Robert seemed like a man led further and further into an engulfing bog:

[*Irish News*: 'Taylor studied for a few moments and then replied'] 'Well, I suppose that's right.'

'Well, I was lying on some side.'

'Well, there has been a strain on me in this court.'

Curran concluded this part of his cross-examination by remarking acidly: 'The reason for your difficulty in giving details of this incident is that it never occurred at all.' Obviously, he felt it unnecessary to add the polite, conventional formula, 'I suggest that . . .'. Hanna meanwhile watched with his elbows resting on the table, his fingertips joined and meeting at his nose, his eyes thoughtful; he was thinking how best to gloss for the jury's benefit the feebleness of his client's performance under this cross-examination.

Cross-examined about his claim to have visited The Daisy, Robert's tendency to embroider his lies for the sake of verisimilitude produced a contradiction which must have greatly embarrassed his counsel while at the same time merely emphasising the falsity of the claim. He said that he gave Clarke a threepenny bit and Clarke gave him two pence change, and that he had a conversation with him, asking him to keep the paper and agreeing to call back for it at six o'clock when Clarke said he would not be busy. Curran promptly reminded him that he had never before made mention of this conversation. He reminded him also that his own counsel had already sought to discredit Clarke's denial that he came to the Daisy that day by suggesting that he must have left the shop for a few minutes to visit the toilet when Robert called. What had he to say to that? 'Well, I was there', was the feeble reply. Later, too, when he said he had arranged to see Billie Booth in The Deer's Head on Saturday night at six, the judge intervened to ask: 'But wasn't that the time you had arranged to go back and see the newsagent?' His answer to this question threw a little light into the moral void of his mind: 'Yes, but it was Clarke who made that appointment.'

Questioned about his financial situation on the morning of the assault, Robert let slip the fact that he had lost most of his money (£15) at the dogs on Thursday night. Most people had worked out by now why this young Protestant bought the Catholic *Irish News* every day; nevertheless, his public admission that he was a reckless gambler was of some use to the prosecution case. But Curran did not dwell on this weakness, for it constituted an affinity between himself and the young criminal he was pushing towards the gallows: he too was a serious gambler, and one whose losses were a domestic problem (a fact sometimes noted in relation to his own dark story, to be considered later here in the Appendix). He concentrated rather on Robert's claim that his appeal to Morrison for the loan of £20 took place in the afternoon, after the assault, rather than in the morning: his argument that desperation for money drove Robert to Ponsonby that morning remained central to his case, and although his argument did not actually depend on a morning visit to Morrison, nevertheless it was strengthened by it – in his view, rejection by Morrison was the psychological 'last straw' for Robert, the collapse of all hope. In his opening address, he again said that 'there would be evidence to prove that on the morning the attack took place Taylor had endeavoured to borrow £20 from a publican'. It is doubtful whether he thought that Morrison would recover his original certainty on this matter; but he clearly intended to direct attention to his shiftiness. When Morrison was brought to the witness box, he did not accuse him of departing from what he said in his statement to the police in April and in the June hearing, but he harried him in a manner which made that fact perfectly clear to judge and jury.

Unfortunately for him, however, and fortunately for Robert, Morrison now went so far as to give credence to the evidence of Mary Erskine that she was with Robert during his alleged afternoon visit. Erskine claimed that she stood in the hall of the pub while Robert spoke to Morrison inside and Morrison now agreed – not that there was much certainty in his evidence on this point. Cross-examined by Fox, the junior defence counsel, about the figure in the hall, he said. 'I don't know whether it was a girl', but when questioned later by Curran, he said: 'There was a girl waiting in the hall . . . there was a girl standing in the hall.' (Did someone's warning eye catch his before he said this?) To help him, defence counsel Fox intervened and asked

Erskine to step forward for identification, and he agreed that she was the girl in the hall. Curran then asked him what she wore when he saw her and he replied, 'I don't know, I took no notice of her.' How then could he identify her so easily in court, six months later? At this point Hanna jumped to the rescue, objecting that Curran was cross-examining and seeking to discredit his own (prosecution) witness – something, of course, which only the defence could do. The objection was upheld and Morrison – whose answers, as the judge complained, were at times barely audible – was released from his misery. However, in his charge to the jury at the close of the trial, the judge would ignore Morrison's tactical uncertainty and quote him as saying 'that on Saturday morning 16 April, the defendant asked for a loan of £20'. Here was one example of external pressure that failed.

In his cross-examination of Mary Erskine, Curran was no less severe, and he was more successful in his attempt to discredit her than he had been in July. Was it not true, he asked her, that she had been married eight years ago? (Someone had been doing useful research.) She agreed that that was so. But in her effort to persuade Mr Williamson to allow a postponement of payment, did she not tell him that she had hired her wedding taxis from him eight months ago and paid for them? This she denied. 'But you heard Mr Williamson giving his evidence to-day, did you not?' asked Curran. To which she replied (as if this disposed of the problem), 'I wasn't listening.' This reply licensed a moment of light relief in the tense proceedings; laughter ran through the court. But Curran had scored a point which gave extra force to his sceptical interrogation of her claim to have gone with Robert to Morrison's in the afternoon.

The prosecution case was so well presented that Hanna had an even more difficult task on hand when he came to address the jury than in the first trial. He began:

At best, gentlemen of the Jury, the Crown case here is that this ordinary young man, little more than a boy, suddenly went mad on the eve of his wedding and committed this horrible crime. For what, gentlemen? What is the motive? Twelve pounds and nine shillings! A few paltry shillings! The Crown case, in my submission, is preposterous! Had he been in such need before his wedding, is it not obvious that any one of his friends in Ponsonby Avenue would have helped him? That charming lady Miss Brennan, whom you have all seen in the witness box, would certainly not have turned him away empty-handed if he had gone to her for help. So why should he murder poor Mrs McGowan?

Two of the most conspicuous tactics in Hanna's lengthy address were apparent here. He presented himself as the voice of plain common sense and flattered the jury as sensible, mature, experienced men of the world. They were men who could be expected not only to see the inherent preposterousness of the Crown case but also to treat with scepticism the arguments of learned men who lived and worked in laboratories and were brought out by the police to support improbable arguments. Like him, the jury could easily pick holes in scientific evidence which, for example, had failed to take account of the fact that although Mary McGowan's hair was a mixture of sandy and white, no sandy hairs were found on Robert's clothing. They too, like him, would have noted that 'none of Robert's hairs were found on her clothing'. And in deciding whether blood could fall from the nose to the ankle while a man was seated on the toilet, 'Dr Firth is no more an expert in such matters than you, gentlemen, or me.'

The other rhetorical feature of this address was a redoubled emphasis on Robert's youthfulness, which had the twin value of strengthening the improbability argument and creating a generally sympathetic attitude to the defendant. The address contained several parenthetical and seemingly instinctive allusions to his extreme youth (as in 'this boy's coat'), but the emphasis was most apparent in dealing with Taylor's performance under cross-examination; typically, Hanna here sought to make a positive out of a negative. 'It is not surprising,' he said, 'that Robert Taylor was not such a good witness' when severely cross-examined by a distinguished and experienced advocate such as the Attorney General: 'He is not a bright, intelligent, keen-brained man. He is a young man on the verge of life. He did not attach any importance to his nose-bleeding.' Indeed, when you came to think of it, he didn't do too badly at all under cross-examination, 'being little more than a boy'.

If the jury was in danger of being taken in by Hanna's virtuoso display of honest-to-God conviction and warm-hearted commitment to the boy's plight, Judge James Andrews prevented that from happening. Andrews was a Grand Master of the Orange Order, but if anyone had tried, however indirectly or remotely, to bring influence to bear on him in this context, it would have been a great mistake. For he was also the Lord Chief Justice and for him that fact took precedence over all others. He had reached the top of his profession and had nothing to lose; he could go no higher, and his professional pride was clearly involved in a sordid case which should have been over and done with months ago. He had not been impressed in the least by Hanna's multitudinous citations of eighteenth- and nineteenth-century cases relevant or barely relevant to his strenuous argument that Mary McGowan's evidence should be discounted (yes, this ground had to be gone over again). And now, in his charge to the jury, and with great lucidity, he confronted them with the plain implications of the evidence presented by the prosecution while drawing attention to the partiality and inconsistencies in the evidence presented by the defence.

It was a masterly blend of objectivity and guidance; he seemed
to lead his hearers to a conclusion by simply, as it were, letting
the facts speak for themselves.

After his opening remarks, he drew attention to the relative
credibility of the prosecution and defence witnesses. It was his
duty, he said, to point out that 'the accused, and at least many of
his witnesses, were interested parties'. The jury should ask
themselves whether the Crown witnesses were shaken:

> By that, I mean, gentlemen, you will decide as jury-
> men not merely upon the words that fall from the lips
> of the witnesses but you will take into account their
> demeanour in the box, from which you can very often
> tell even better than from words, whether the words
> that have been uttered are truthful or not. I repeat
> then, you will ask yourselves were the Crown wit-
> nesses shaken under the skilful cross-examination of
> Mr Hanna and of Mr Fox? There can be no doubt . . .
> that the accused's witnesses were shaken. At any
> rate, the accused himself was shaken when he had to
> admit the lies that he told and when he further went
> on and said that the lies were told to deceive, and to
> deceive the police.

Hanna had closed his address to the jury by listing eight
questions which the jury had to answer in attempting to reach a
verdict. The questions in effect contained Hanna's answers and
gave the impression that he was wrapping up the case in an argument endowed with mathematical certainty. Without seeming
obviously ironical, the judge alluded politely to these eight
questions (the politeness of lawyers is almost always ironical)
and said he could see 'at least ten other questions' which he
thought were worthy the gentlemens' attention. He then listed
the ten:

Why did the accused say, if he is innocent, that Booth owed him five pounds? The answer comes in his own words: 'To deceive the police.'

Why did he wish to deceive the police, if he is innocent? The truth is good enough.

Why did he make the false statement . . . about The Daisy?

Could a drop of blood from the nose, in your opinion, and having regard to our knowledge of human affairs, penetrate two pairs of socks and trickle down the instep of the foot, not merely in one but in three different directions?

Where is it most likely that the cereal found by Dr Firth came from, if not from the kitchen in 18 Ponsonby Avenue, which was covered and bespattered with the barley from the soup that was spilt over the head of this wretched woman?

Is Mrs Shiels – an honest, disinterested and impartial lady who would not wish to see an innocent man convicted (as I suggest to you) – telling a lie, or, as the only alternative, is she mistaken?

Why did the accused tell the police that the bloodstains were paint and now tell us that they came from nose-bleeding *on the very day before*?

Do you accept that a young man would pull an overcoat over him in a kitchen which he says was warm?

He said he was lying on his left side and then said he was lying on his right side. How could he allow so many drops of blood fall on his coat when his handkerchief was immediately within his reach and was subsequently procured by his own hand? Is it customary when noses bleed to let them bleed on over-

coats, which nowadays are precious garments, when
the blood could be stopped quickly and absorbed by a
handkerchief, which can easily be washed?

A smaller point: Did a little child make the five
scratches upon his face which were unquestionably
fresh scratches? Five – not one, but five. And when
asked about them his answer was not, 'The child did
it', but, 'It could have been done by the child'.

Finally, the most important question of all. Did Mrs
McGowan, that poor lady, tell the truth when she declared on four different occasions, 'Robert did it'; and
gave, moreover, the details of how he did it, which
precisely corresponded, as I suggest to you, with the
nature of the injuries which she received? Was she
mistaken? Counsel says it was a question of mistaken
identity. The assailant grasped her by the throat; she
had no opportunity of seeing who it was. But according to her, she opened the door and the accused entered and spoke to her and asked for the liberty to use
her telephone. It was only then that, according to her,
the attack was made upon her. I suggest to you that at
that early stage at any rate, she was not distraught and
had the opportunity of seeing full well who he was
who entered her house. And you will not forget too
that, according to her story, if it is true, she had seen
him outside only ten minutes before.

Then, with a solemnity befitting the occasion, and with a
subtly modulated contrast between the voice of the dead woman
and the rhetorical bravura of the defence lawyer, the judge concluded thus:

The voice that has spoken to us in these dying decla-
rations was the voice of Mary McGowan, sitting as
she then was, on the edge of eternity; and today, gen-

tlemen, it is for you to say, Is not her voice still cry-
ing to us from the grave, for justice? The question,
however, is not for me to answer. I have a heavy duty
to discharge in this case, but the ultimate verdict is
yours. Mr Hanna appealed to you with all the force at
his command. That is an issue that you will decide
for yourselves. Who is right?

The Clerk of the Crown and Peace then swore a policeman
to keep the jury. The issue paper on which the verdict would be
written was handed to the foreman and at 3.56 pm the jury retired to consider their verdict.

*

Would it be another marathon session, an agonised tussle behind
closed doors? Most people thought not. For all his emphasis on
the right of the jury to decide, the Lord Chief Justice himself
had made it clear that he wanted a guilty verdict; and who
would dare to resist him? Robert's group of relatives and friends
– he would glance in their direction from time to time in the trial
– looked grim. Yet he himself did not; strangely, he seemed to
have recovered from his battering of the day before, and he had
listened today with an air almost of detachment to the damning
analyses in Curran's address to the jury and in the judge's
charge. A character who hitherto had seemed a puzzle to so
many now seemed more than that: an enigma.

Exactly nine minutes after the jury retired, the usual buzz
and babble in the court was suddenly stilled when the judge re-
appeared to say that a message had come from the jury asking to
see the bloodstained coat and jacket. These exhibits were then
carried out by a warder, and the buzz and babble resumed at a
higher pitch: the stained clothes seemed to betoken the end, the
inescapable signature of guilt. Then at 4.35 pm the jury returned: they had been out only thirty-nine minutes.

Robert was escorted into the court by two warders just as the jury were filling their places. When he entered the dock, observed the *Irish News* reporter, 'he rubbed his hands and smiled at a warder immediately beside him' (and with whom he had been exchanging some words on the way in). When all were settled and the court quiet, the jury foreman handed the issue paper to the clerk, who called out in a loud voice: 'How say you Mr Foreman, is the prisoner, Robert Taylor, guilty of the wilful murder of Mary McGowan, of which he stands charged?' And back came the answer from Mr Woods, 'Guilty, my Lord.'

'Taylor received the sentence without the least perturbation,' observed the *Irish News* man. He did not grip the sides of the box and stand stiffly as at the end of the first trial, his features did not contract, he did not moisten his lips, his breathing could not be heard, his head did not sink. He stood upright and relaxed and looked at one with his white open-necked shirt and his blue suit.

It was the judge whose countenance registered pain and fear of what was to be. Addressing Robert, he said that he had been found guilty of 'a brutal and callous murder upon not merely convincing but conclusive evidence'. And he continued: 'I do not wish to add to the pain and anguish of the moment for you, which indeed must be great. I shall therefore content myself with simply pronouncing the dread judgment and sentence of the Court as ordained by law.' Then he looked at the clerk and his head declined for more than a few seconds as the black cap was placed on it. Raising his head slowly, as if reluctantly, and looking down at the calm face of Robert Taylor, he said:

> The sentence and judgment of the Court is and it is hereby ordered and adjudged that you, Robert Taylor, be taken from the bar of the Court where you now stand to . . . His Majesty's prison, and that on Wednesday, the 16th day of November, in the year of

Our Lord One Thousand Nine Hundred and Forty-Nine, you be taken to the common place of execution in the prison and there hanged by the neck until you are dead; and that your body be buried within the walls of the prison in which the said judgment of death shall be executed on you. And may the Lord have mercy on your soul.

As Robert was being led from the Court, an awed silence was broken by a woman's scream. Robert paused for a moment and looked in the direction of the doors to the vestibule where his pregnant girlfriend had sat since early morning.

Experienced crime reporters and lawyers were taken aback by the twenty-one-year-old's demeanour at the end of this trial, and all the more so when they remembered his understandable distress near the close of the first trial. The aristocratic heroes of tragic and romantic literature behave with stoic flair in the face of execution, and the political and religious martyrs of history often sought to meet their end with quiet dignity. But history has shown that ordinary mortals make no display of indifference when faced with the prospect of violent extinction. One explanation for Robert's behaviour might be that he was making, for the benefit of his friends, a desperate show of bravado which he knew perfectly well would not be possible on the morning he was led handcuffed from the condemned cell to the hanging place. But there is another and more likely explanation for his apparent fearlessness: it is embedded in the circumstances behind Hanna's appeal against the sentence; an explanation reinforced by a reliable witness's account of Robert's behaviour when housed in the condemned cell – but we mustn't get ahead of ourselves.

19

RALPH STUART NEILSON WAS under-sheriff of Belfast and one of the city's leading solicitors. In his capacity as under-sheriff he was responsible for the care and conduct of the jury at Robert's two trials. On the Wednesday morning of the second trial (notes *The Northern Ireland Law Reports* for 1950), he approached Judge Andrews before the court sat with a request from the jury: they were feeling the effects of the prolonged court sittings and they asked if they might be allowed to go that evening to Bangor (a seaside resort some twelve miles away) for fresh air and exercise. Reminded by Neilson that a similar request had been granted by Judge Sheil at the July trial, Andrews assented. Neilson did not say whether the present jury knew that their predecessors had been granted this liberty, and if so who had informed them. Nor did he mention whether or not the said liberty had led to any irregularity (unintentional or otherwise) in July; but of course any attempt on the part of the defence to gain something by exposing an irregularity after the July trial would have been rendered superfluous by the Crown's failure to convict. Conscious, however, of the dangers inherent in any relaxation of the rules, Judge Andrews (as he was careful to explain later) 'assented to the request on the *express instructions* that the jury should be accompanied by at least four members of the Royal Ulster Constabulary (one of whom should be of at least sergeant rank)', and that, as he again *'expressly stated, the body of jurors should be both immediately preceded and immediately followed on their walk by two policemen to prevent any possibility of irregularity'* (italics added). On these conditions the four jury keepers were duly sworn in at the end of the day's proceedings in court. One did not have to be a trained lawyer with experience in the conduct and care of juries to see what this meant; an illiterate would have instantly inferred that the jurors were not to be allowed to separate. The geometry of the required arrangement was self-explanatory.

The four RUC men chosen for this duty were Sergeant J. Rouse and Constables John Montgomery, Thomas Stewart and Robert Malcolm; and it may not be irrelevant to note that they were based at the Leopold Street barracks and not Glenravel Street, the station which had devoted so much of its time to putting together the case against Taylor; had the jury keepers been Glenravel men, the history of Robert the Painter might have had a different ending.

The *Northern Ireland Law Reports'* account of the jury's quest for fresh air follows verbatim the account given in sworn affidavits provided by the RUC men after the trial ended. The bus left the Courthouse at about 7.15, but before the party mounted, the foreman of the jury, Mr John Woods, instructed the driver not to stop at Bangor but to drive on to Donaghadee. Here was a minor infringement of the judge's conditions; a grave infringement was to follow. On arrival in Donaghadee at about 8.00 pm, the party immediately separated, breaking up into three groups and going off in different directions. The sergeant (like the constables, he was dressed in plain clothes) joined a group of six jurymen and on the suggestion of Mr Woods they entered a public house. Here they occupied a room in which two men were already drinking, but these soon left and no words were exchanged with them. The seven had three rounds of drinks ('including some minerals', added the sergeant pointedly) and returned to the bus at about 9.00 pm. Constable Malcolm had joined a group of three jurymen who went for a walk along the pier towards the lighthouse; they returned to the bus after about ten minutes, having found the weather uninviting. For the same reason, they were soon joined by Constables Stewart and Montgomery and their group of three. All then went off to a café on the sea front for tea. When they were in the café, the Taylor case was not discussed and no one there apart from the person who served the tea spoke to them. The entire party regrouped at 9.00 pm and were back in the Courthouse one hour later.

Next morning the judge in friendly fashion asked the under-sheriff if the trip had been a success and was informed that indeed it had; 'the jury had much appreciated the consideration I had shown them,' he would report later. On the following night (Thursday), a second trip took place, without permission having been sought from him and without him being subsequently informed of it. We do not know whether the under-sheriff was consulted about the second trip and if so whether he presumed he could take the judge's permission for granted, or whether the policemen were sworn in for the occasion. Nor do we know if the under-sheriff was aware that the travellers had broken up into three parties. But if he was and if he had known that a second unauthorised journey had taken place, and if he had mentioned either of these facts to the judge, then the judge, as he said later, would have been prepared to stop the trial immediately, ask for a new jury and order a retrial.

The destination of the second trip, again chosen by the foreman, was Antrim, an inland town some twenty miles from Belfast: no beauty spot, but well away from the rough winds that were buffeting the coast. This time, the process of separation occurred at the point of departure, for three jurymen elected to stay behind, and one policeman perforce remained with them. On arrival at Antrim, the party again broke up into three groups. At the foreman's suggestion, the sergeant and three jurymen went for a drink in Hall's Hotel. Here they found a room already occupied by a man and two women, who left shortly afterwards without exchanging words with them. Constable Malcolm and three jurymen walked up the main street and then back to a café near Hall's, where they had coffee and pastry; while they were there, one stranger exchanged words with them about the weather, but apart from that there was no talk with outsiders and they left after about ten minutes. Constable Stewart and his group walked up the street too but went into a shop at the request of one juryman who wanted to buy pears. There were three women and a man in the shop and conversation with them took place. One of the jurymen was recognised by the woman in charge of the shop; she had not seen him for fifteen years and they talked about mutual friends. The other two jurymen conversed with the remaining two women and the man, the talk being mostly about tea, as the stranger worked for a tea firm. Nothing was said that had any bearing on the Taylor case. They then went for a walk towards the station and visited Hall's Hotel, where they had a round of drinks in the lounge, leaving after about twenty minutes. Except when drinks were ordered, no conversation took place with anyone there and the Taylor case was not discussed.

On the return journey a slight deviation from the normal route took place when Woods directed the driver to turn off Antrim Road into Limestone Road and return by way of Atlantic Avenue, passing Baltic Avenue on the right and Ponsonby on the left; but although this was the scene of the crime, the Taylor case, says the *Law Reports* (quoting the affidavits), was not discussed.

20

WHILE THE JURY'S EVENING jaunts were taking place, George Hanna was hard at work preparing for the last two days of the trial. Although his efforts failed, the extent of his commitment was duly recognised, and not just by the judge. The Stormont seat for Duncairn, the Tiger's Bay constituency, had fallen vacant at the end of August with the death of its Unionist incumbent, William Grant. Hanna was invited by the local Unionist party to stand for the seat and he did so, winning it handsomely in the by-election of 29 November. In the process, he subjected the Labour candidate to yet another humiliating defeat, being seen himself in Tiger's Bay as the champion of the little man, 'our Robert'.

One might have thought that after the second trial, and even when the by-election was pending, he would have considered he had done enough on behalf of someone whom he and everyone else knew had committed what the Lord Chief Justice had called 'a brutal and callous murder' and that he would have been content (if not pleased) to let the law take its course. But that apparently was not the case. The trial ended on Friday 28 October. On the following Monday, and to widespread surprise (given the manifest soundness of the verdict), the defence announced that it would appeal against the sentence. Hanna's weapon in the appeal was the set of sworn affidavits from the jury foreman and from the four RUC men, explaining in full and unembarrassed detail what they had done on their trips to Donaghadee and Antrim. These affidavits were collected by the solicitor Anthony Lunn, who had been provided with information about the irregularities by a person or persons now unknown. Hanna (and presumably the person or persons unknown) knew that the Northern Ireland Criminal Law Act of 1945 would allow him to demand setting aside the verdict on the ground of jury separation; and he knew too that if he succeeded, Robert Taylor, having had a full and satisfactory trial, and not a 'nullity', could not be tried again (*de novo*, as the jargon went). The murderer would go free on a technicality and the voice of the dead woman appealing for justice would be mocked by the law. From Hanna's perspective, the jurymen and their keepers were not passing the time idly in Donaghadee and Antrim. Unwittingly or otherwise, they were elaborately ensuring that his efforts on Robert's behalf would not fail. It is a curious though perhaps insignificant fact that the possibility of frustrating the proper outcome of a murder trial by means of a technicality had been on Hanna's mind in his address to the jury at the close of the second trial when (in spite of the Lord Chief Justice's ruling) he told the jury that acceptance of a dying person's evidence without resort to cross-examination was 'a legal technicality'.

He was granted leave to appeal. Less than three weeks after he had become MP for Duncairn, and less than a week before Christmas, he began his third attempt to save the life of his constituent's fiancé. Over a period of four days, he argued his case with characteristic energy and panache before two appeal judges, Lord Justice Porter and Lord Justice Black. His old antagonist Lancelot Curran had been made a High Court judge and consequently had withdrawn from politics, his place in the appeal court being taken by the new Attorney General, J.E. Warnock, KC, MP, assisted, like his predecessor, by W.F. McCoy, KC, MP. It was an intimate legal tussle where the two Lord Justices felt relaxed enough to exchange some learned and insensitive banter on the subject of hanging.

Again, the court was crowded each day; like the Linfield-Celtic conflict, this contest now had its following of committed spectators who would follow it to the last. Among them as usual was Taylor's father, who sat hunched at the end of the front row. He followed the four-day argument from beginning to end and looked dazed as well as apprehensive while George Hanna led his colleagues through a labyrinth of cases and authorities stretching from Ireland, England and Wales to Australia, and from 1949 back through each preceding century to the reign of Henry VII. Another observer was the indefatigable *Irish News* man, who would provide his paper's readers with a fuller account of the proceedings than the *Northern Ireland Law Reports* would give the legal profession (and whose identity, alas, is unknown). It was probably due to this experienced observer's ironic scepticism and disillusioned prescience that his account

of the first day's proceedings, headed, 'Taylor Appeals Against
The Death Sentence', was printed conspicuously side-by-side
with a short item headed, 'When the Crowd Shouted He Let The
Thief Escape'. It began:

> Joseph Green, a packer, said at Belfast Custody Court
> yesterday that he allowed a man who had carried a
> box out of his firm's premises to escape when a
> crowd gathered round. Some shouted, 'Let him go,
> it's near Christmas.'

The timing of Taylor's appeal against the death sentence – it
ended three days before Christmas – was fortuitous. But pressure on court proceedings from the crowd had never been a
chance happening.

Hanna's case for setting aside the sentence was based on the
claim that it was wrong to admit the dying woman's declaration
as evidence and on the fact that the jury had separated during the
trial. That he believed there was any hope of disqualifying Mary
McGowan's evidence is very doubtful, now that it had been discussed at length and accepted by two judges, including the Lord
Chief Justice; at any rate, most of his energy was devoted to the
separation issue, and it was this aspect of the appeal that the appeal judges took very seriously. Perhaps the most remarkable
feature of the whole appeal procedure occurred at the start, when
a gentlemanly agreement was reached that in discussing the
separation issue it would be sufficient to draw on the sworn affidavits of the four RUC men 'as agreed statements of fact: there
would be no need to call witnesses' (to quote Porter). Thus three
Unionist MPs and two members of the Orange Order's Grand
Lodge Committee (Porter and Black) decided that in whatever
direction the inquiry might go, and whatever their professional
disagreements in evaluating the available evidence might be,

they would not submit the RUC men and the jury foreman to awkward questions as to why they behaved as they did.

Hanna began by reading out the four policemen's affidavits in their entirety. He then opened his case by objecting to a minor aspect of the separation process, namely the fact that on the second outing nine of the jurors, by virtue of passing along Atlantic Avenue, had effectively formed themselves into a 'view' jury, 'drawing conclusions from what they saw which were not available to the other three jurors'. In making this point, he was the first to render explicit the court's determination to ensure that no blame should attach to anyone for what had happened: 'I am not suggesting,' he remarked, 'that any juror did anything deliberately wrong, but there was an impropriety', an 'irregularity', since there was a deviation from their legislature's rule that in cases of treason, treason felony and murder a jury could not separate until they had brought in a verdict. Separation meant to divide into different parts and here was a case of division into three parties. Separation was 'inherently wrong and must not be tolerated' because it gave rise to the possibility of tampering with the jury. 'I am not suggesting that there was any tampering,' he added, but 'it was clear from the evidence of the affidavits that there was opportunity for tampering'; moreover, 'the law did not require evidence of misconduct on the part of the jury'. It was true, he agreed, that a jury keeper was present with each of the three groups, but jury keepers 'are only human beings and not all-seeing and all-hearing' and they could not have been certain that the trial was not discussed when the jurors spoke to members of the public (his avoidance at all times of reference to the jurykeepers as policemen was technically correct, of course, but it happily conspired with the hands-off-the-police attitude so apparent in the whole procedure).

More than once, Hanna spoke in tones of heartfelt indignation against the wrong that would be done to his client, to the legal profession and to society at large if a verdict based on such a trial were allowed to stand. A breach of the jurykeeper's oath not to allow the jury to separate had taken place, and that being so, 'Robert Taylor did not have the protection of the essential rules of procedure'; an 'injustice' had been done. 'Every person connected with the case must have cause for discomfort and must feel that there was something wrong' if the verdict was allowed to stand; 'it would be unseemly that any court should be asked to sanction, approve, or even permit the conduct that took place in this case.' It was an issue that 'goes to the root of our criminal procedure. Never at any time in the history of the administration of justice has the general public been so convinced of the freedom of the courts from outside influence.' The irony of these protestations, which could more easily be invoked against the outcome Hanna was advocating, seems not to have been observed by any of the lawyers present.

Warnock's style, by contrast, was matter-of-fact and commonsensical. The jury's decision to drive past the scene of the crime was 'a trivial matter' prompted by curiosity alone – 'that was as plain as a pikestaff'. It was dark at the time, the bus did not stop and they could not have formed any opinion; these facts showed that it was entirely wrong to attach any importance to the incident. On the larger issue, the affidavits made clear that the jurors' communication with the outside public did not touch on the case; no one disputed that fact. The mere possibility of prejudice to the jury was not enough to justify the verdict being upset. Admittedly there was a departure from normal and correct procedure, and no one would wish to approve of that; but it did not constitute a ground of mis-trial. It had not been shown that the irregularities which occurred had affected the jury's verdict or their mind; on the contrary, there was an abundance of evidence that they had not. In order to quash the sentence, the court must be satisfied that there was a miscarriage of justice, and unless they were so satisfied they must dismiss the appeal. 'And there is overwhelming evidence,' he insisted, 'that there was no miscarriage of justice.' That there might be such if the verdict was set aside is a point he did not raise.

Common sense and common practice suggest that three appeal judges are more desirable than two: if there is a difference of opinion in the latter case, the senior judge or stronger personality is always liable to dictate the outcome. It would have been difficult to predict from their performance in court which of the two appeal judges in the Taylor case would be the more determined in ensuring that his view prevailed. However, one could infer from their interventions that Black was considerably more in sympathy with Warnock's position than was Porter, the senior appeal judge. When Hanna in one of his more heated moments declared that 'separation was inherently wrong' and 'will not be tolerated,' Black commented mildly (though with the mildness of Pontius Pilate): 'The Attorney General says it may be undesirable but not wrong.' And when Hanna talked about injustice to Taylor he observed: 'An agreed statement of the facts shows that nothing prejudicial to your client happened – that is the argument of the Attorney General.' Porter's comments, however, tended to chime with Hanna's sentiment that the irregularities of the case were so extraordinary (a jury 'running around in wee bits and pieces in Donaghadee and Antrim', said Hanna) that legal historians in future ages would not forgive this Court if it were seen to have tolerated anything so unseemly; a sentiment which tended to make Taylor's proven guilt a matter of incidental significance. 'The issues in this case are wide and serious,' intoned Porter, signifying agreement with Hanna ; and he asked wonderingly: 'Has there ever been a case in which a similar thing occurred?' Hanna, who had already been at pains to display his familiarity with the remote corners of legal history, replied: 'I have been able to find no such sug-

gestion.' That grave reply, and his more resounding phrase,
'Never at any time in the history of the administration of justice
. . .' seemed to touch Porter's reverence for the judicial past. He
(and not Black) announced at the end of the fourth day's proceedings that this was a 'most difficult case' and that judgment
in consequence would have to be reserved until after Christmas.
To him, nothing seemed plain as a pikestaff.

And perhaps he was hearing subliminal voices cry, 'Let him
go, it's near Christmas!'

21

S AMUEL CLARKE PORTER (1875–1956) had been a brilliant
student at Queen's University, Belfast, where he gained a
first in Classics before going on to take the Ll.B, when he again
distinguished himself. An academic career might have beck-
oned, a Holdsworth Fellowship in Legal History at Oxford perhaps; but he chose to practise law and even veered towards politics. In 1920, he stood as a Labour candidate for East Belfast,
though without success. He might never have succeeded in the
law to the extent that he did had he not relinquished his socialist
affiliations and embraced Orangeism. Now, at the age of sev-
enty-six, and probably the most respected as well as the most
amiable member of his profession in Ulster, he seemed to approach 'this most difficult case' with a scholarly determination
to make his mark in legal history by being seen to have defined
its intricacies and implications with authoritative fullness. But it
was as if his scholarly preoccupation with the oddities of the
case was a means by which he could blind himself and others to
its essentials.

He delivered the ruling at the Court of Appeal on 20 January, with Judge Black sitting silently beside him. It was unquestionably the most momentous day in his long career; the day

when his wisdom and erudition would conclusively end the most discussed and most suspenseful murder case in Ulster history. The interest of the general public was more remarkable than ever, as would be apparent that evening when the sales of the city's only evening paper, *The Belfast Telegraph,* far outstripped previous records. Crowds gathered from early morning and thronged the grounds of the Court and the road outside. There was an unusually strong police presence, uniformed and in plain clothes, backed by radio cars, both at the Court and at well-known flashpoints in different parts of the city. No one now questioned the sectarian significance of the case. When the proceedings in the Court of Appeal commenced at 10.00 am, the public gallery was crowded and every seat in the well of the court and the press box was occupied. People stood along each side of the Court, too, and gathered round the doors as well. There was complete silence when at 10.05 the two judges took their seats. Porter turned to the Registrar and said: 'Call the case, please.' He did so, Porter began and – remarkably – his seventy-minute speech was heard throughout in hushed silence.

He commenced by rejecting the defence submission that the trial judge wrongly admitted evidence from a dying declaration and gave most of his attention to the issue of jury separation. He began this part of his analysis by reading out a report from the trial judge in which he recalled the terms of his 'express instructions' and his ignorance of the irregularities which took place on both evenings. In a carefully coded message indicating where he stood on the appeal, the Lord Chief Justice concluded that 'even if any irregularity did take place, I cannot believe that any of them [the jurors] would have discussed the case with any other than members of their own body': meaning that the essential purpose of the separation rule had not been vitiated and that in consequence the sentence should stand. Porter made no comment on this element of the Lord Chief Justice's letter.

After giving an account of the two evening trips (based on the policemen's affidavits), he surveyed the history of the separation rule, referring to all the authorities and cases cited by Hanna and Warnock, adding a few of his own and commenting meticulously on each. He noted the initial severity of the rule, when juries were locked up and denied food and drink until they reached a verdict, and traced its modifications and relaxations down the centuries until the point where in England since 1940 the jurors were allowed to go their separate ways at the end of each day *before* the judge summed up and they retired to deliberate (after which they could not separate or communicate with anyone else). But he did not dwell on current English practice and went on to emphasise that the position in Northern Ireland was unchanged since the Juries Detention Act of 1897, according to which, in a trial for murder, treason or treason felony, no jury could separate either before or after the judge sums up.

Porter accepted the view of both judges in the Taylor case that it was not inconsistent with the 1897 rule to allow the jury to be taken out to the country or the seaside for fresh air and exercise, provided of course that permission was granted, that separation was ruled out and that the entire group was in the care of sworn jury keepers. Where he differed from the Crown counsel on the Taylor appeal was mainly in the significance he attached to the consequences of separation and the various irregularities in this particular case. But despite the scrupulosity with which he argued his case and the heavy weight of erudition he brought to it, his reasoning was by no means flawless.

Dealing, for example, with the Crown counsel's point that there is no rule of law that members of a 'locked up' jury may not hold communication with outsiders during an adjournment in the course of the trial (i.e. before the summing up), provided that the jury keepers see to it that any such communications do not relate to the subject matter of the case, he responded with what we might call 'the unacceptable consequence' argument, a rhetorical device borrowed from Hanna which he used quite often. If Crown counsel's principle were accepted, he maintained, 'it would mean that members of a locked up jury could freely receive visitors from the outside, provided that the visits were in the presence of a jury keeper'. This implies that the court and jury keepers would have no wish or need or right to exercise strict control over the number of 'visitors' or interlocutors, or to limit the circumstances when such encounters should take place – which is entirely incorrect. The word 'freely' is gratuitous, the concomitant hint of anarchy tendentious.

Commenting on the (to him) 'strange' fact that 'there is little authority to be found in the law reports with regard to the keeping of a jury prior to the judge's charge', he turned for help to a case unearthed by Hanna, that of *R. v. Murphy*, and applied it to the case now in question. In the Murphy case, after a conviction for murder, the Supreme Court of New South Wales set aside the conviction and granted a *venire de novo* for the retrial of the accused on the ground that the jury, while locked up during the trial, had access to newspapers containing reports of the trial so far as it had gone. The court, in its judgments, held that the effect of this was to create an extreme risk of a miscarriage of justice. The Judicial Committee reversed this decision but indicated that the irregularity complained of was such as might justifiably have been made a ground of appeal if there had been in New South Wales at that time a court invested with the powers of the English and Northern Irish Court of Criminal Appeal. *Ergo*, argued Porter, counsel for Taylor had ground for appeal against the verdict. But the Murphy case was hardly analogous; there is a great difference between a juror (a) asking for a pound of pears and (b) privately devouring what the newspapers had to say on the murder case which concerned him. Porter sought to get round this problem several minutes later when commenting on the jurors' visit to the shop in Antrim: 'What more natural than that one or two of them might buy newspapers containing reports of the case?' To which he added (almost turning a *might* which he knew did not materialise into a *fact*): 'It is to be remembered that it was upon the fact that the jury had access to newspaper reports that the Supreme Court of New South Wales based their judgments in *R. v. Murphy*.'

Conversion of possibility into something as substantial as fact constituted the basis of Porter's argument, and here again he was taking his cue from Hanna. The jury, he agreed, did not do what would unquestionably have violated the principle determining the separation rule, but they might have done it. The key word in his discourse here was 'opportunity'. 'The evidence no doubt is that while in Donaghadee and Antrim they did not discuss the trial with any person whom they met there. But they *certainly* had opportunities of doing so which they ought not to have had.' (In this suggestive rhetorical trope, hypothesis slides into certainty, becomes equivalent to 'no doubt'). In the Crown's interpretation of the separation rule, the object of the rule was to guard against tampering with or influencing the jury during the trial; but for Porter, as for Hanna, 'the object of the rule is to guard against opportunities of tampering with or influencing the jury'. One can understand the practical wisdom of this formulation, but to apply it rigidly in all cases, and especially a case such as Taylor's, does not make sense. Moreover, if it were granted absolutely then the relaxations of the rule which Porter himself acknowledged as legitimate (a juror talking briefly on a matter of practical necessity to a jury keeper, a waiter, or a doctor; going to the toilet; going for a walk as a group in public) – these too could be condemned as offering opportunities to the determined and the ingenious for tampering and influencing. What more natural and easy for a waiter or a doctor than to slip a note to a juror in the Taylor case pointing out that the defence's repeated intimation that the accused was a man of unblemished character was false and that he had been a compulsive thief for years?

Porter placed much emphasis on the sheer number of irregularities in the jury's conduct: they made a second trip without proper authorisation; they twice divided into parties, not just two but three parties; they visited a public house, a public restaurant and shops; they spoke to members of the public; they made an unauthorised visit to the scene of the crime. Fact-seeming hypotheses expanded this list so that it began to seem endless: they put themselves in situations which:

> . . . were almost certain to invite questions as to who the passengers were and what was the business which brought them there; and even if members of the jury did not enter into conversation about the case, one could hardly be certain that they would overhear nothing about the topic which was on everybody's lips. Moreover, what more natural . . . ?

The effect of cataloguing the jury's misdemeanours was to confuse quantity with essence: the essential, witnessed fact that they did not discuss the trial with anyone and that no influence was brought to bear on them was not altered by the large number of actual and potential irregularities. For Porter, however, the conclusion was obvious: 'Where there are so many substantial irregularities as have been disclosed by the evidence in this case' – note how shadows have been assimilated to substance – 'the accused person is entitled to complain that his trial has not been conducted according to established and recognised principles of our legal procedure . . . to deprive an accused person of the protection given by essential steps in the criminal procedure constitutes in itself a miscarriage of justice.' In this way, the figure of Robert Taylor as a victim of injustice emerges to displace the voice that the trial judge heard from beyond the grave: Taylor 'might justly ask how was he to test whether or not the jury had heard anything outside which might influence them in their deliberations'. He 'did not receive that measure of protection to which he was entitled according to our law'. The legal process must not be subject to external influence, and be seen not to be so.

But society itself, Porter added, would also be wronged and outraged if what happened in Donaghadee and Antrim were tolerated. Hanna's spirit now seemed in the ascendant, the irony which attended his protestations in December more potent than ever:

> That the due and orderly administration of justice should be maintained is a concern of the whole community . . . it is essential that public confidence in the system of trial by jury in capital cases should not be shaken by any irregularity tending to throw doubt or suspicion upon the reality of the privacy of the jury. It would be disastrous if it was thought that a series of irregularities such as those in the present case could be disregarded. If such an impression was allowed to get abroad the public would look on the locking up of the jury as a vain and useless ceremonial.

And so, concluded Porter, 'on a review of all the facts', he and his colleague had decided that the appeal must be allowed. He added that there could not be another trial. The conviction, he said, was quashed, the prisoner acquitted. Not once did he reveal the slightest regret that his reasoning should have led him to this conclusion; not once did he concede that it could seem in any way unsatisfactory.

An outstanding feature of his judgment was the reiterated claim that although something very damaging had occurred, something grave enough to allow a proven murderer walk free, no one was responsible, no one understood what was going on.

He kept returning to the notion of responsibility as if it were an irritating irrelevance that had to be mentioned but merited no more than parenthetical reference. The tendency appeared at the outset when he began to unfold the tale of multiple improprieties:

> We, of course, entirely accept the assurance of Mr Hanna that neither he nor his colleague, nor the solicitor instructing them, was aware of the alleged separation of the jury until some time after the conclusion of the trial, and that none of them was aware of the actual facts relating to the separation until they had seen the affidavits filed on behalf of the Crown.

Very obviously, the polite 'of course' was not an example of arch, court-room irony (though the *Irish News* man might have murmured 'Of course' to that). It signified unchallengeable truth, and indeed in this instance it may well have been justified. Less justified were the nervous parentheses exonerating the jurors and (although these were not even mentioned) the under-sheriff and the police:

> *By some unfortunate mischance – arising we know not how –* his [the judge's] directions do not appear to have been conveyed either to the jury or the jury-keepers. What was done was clearly outside the authority he gave.

> But *they were obviously not aware* that the permission which he had given was merely to have an opportunity of taking fresh air and exercise together.

> *We do not know how, or why*, it was assumed that the permission to leave the Courthouse on Wednesday evening for a run to Bangor included permission for an outing on Thursday evening also to wherever the jury chose to go.

> In visiting the public houses and cafes, the jurors, *no
> doubt quite unwittingly*, but certainly without any
> permission or authority, had gone completely outside
> the limits which the court had drawn for their proper
> keeping and control.

> [T]he only persons who could give evidence on the
> matter were persons who themselves – *albeit quite
> unconsciously* – were involved in the irregularities.

Porter's pose of helpless ignorance as to causes and of certain
knowledge as to motives and mental states, was disingenuous to
say the least. Looking at 'all the facts', he might have reflected
that if there was a plan to sabotage the trial by overtly violating
the separation rule, and to do so in a manner which protected the
police from the allegation of serious misconduct, it could not have
been devised more skilfully or executed more thoroughly: triple
separation, not just on one but on two nights; the second trip unauthorised; talk with outsiders – but no mention of the trial. It all
looked much too patterned and elaborate to have happened by
pure chance (Robert's Lady Luck furiously at work). Porter chose
the less probable of two possible explanations.

Moreover, he did know, or was wilfully remiss if he did not
know, that whatever the awareness of the police and the jury as
to the significance of what they were doing, a substantial degree
of responsibility for their conduct could be traced back and imputed to at least one person; and if Porter did know this – we
can be almost certain that he did – he was seriously culpable in
not addressing it at the time of the appeal or subsequently.

When the four RUC men submitted their affidavits it would
seem that higher authority intervened to ensure that no responsibility for the debacle would attach to the police force or any of
its members. There had been a Head Constable (John Hunter) on
duty at court and it was to him that the under-sheriff communi-

cated the judge's 'express instructions' about the conduct of the outings. On 15 December 1949, one week after the four men submitted their affidavits, the under-sheriff submitted (at whose request?) an affidavit in which he said that he '*impressed* on the Head Constable the *absolute necessity* of ensuring that no member of the Jury communicated *in any way* with *any member of the public* regarding the case'. The phrasing (italics added here as above) lays claim to an impregnable correctness, but that is in part designed to blunt the significance of the following admission, in which there is an adroit slip from the active to the passive voice: 'but there was no discussion between me and the Head Constable about ensuring that the Jury remained together as a body.' Lest that was insufficient to exonerate the police, the Head Constable on the following day offered an affidavit in which he insisted: 'No mention was made by Mr Neilson about the Jury keeping together.'

Porter saw these affidavits. At the beginning of his allocution, he mentioned 'affidavits to which we need not refer . . . made by the Under-Sheriff of the City, the Clerk of the Crown and Peace, a Head Constable of the Royal Ulster Constabulary and a sergeant and four constables of the same force who had been sworn as jury keepers'. He would accurately summarise for the benefit of his hearers the affidavits of the four jury keepers, but he would tell his hearers that he and Judge Black had no idea whatsoever as to how the four policemen and the jurors failed to follow the judge's express instructions.

It would seem that the trail of lies in this case stretched from Robert Taylor all the way up to the two men who set him free. How many others apart from Porter and Black were knowingly complicit, or acquiesced, in the (deliberate or accidental) sabotaging of the trial one cannot say; but it is hard to believe that the under-sheriff, a solicitor experienced in court rules and jury control, was either so stupid as not to understand the judge's express instructions, or so utterly negligent as to forget them. It is almost equally hard to believe that a sergeant and three constables did not know what they were doing.

In effect, Porter's argument was that the improprieties attendant on the separation process were so shocking ('an affront to the dignity of justice', as defence counsel put it) that it was better to let a proven murderer go unpunished than to tolerate them as a one-off set of infringements whose significance was more apparent than real. In this argument, as in his failure to express regret or hesitation concerning its final outcome, he showed that mentally he was not living in the real world; or that he was determined for the time being not to consider the real world. At that very moment a much headlined murder trial was going on in England where, until the day they withdrew to agree a verdict, the jurors went home every evening and were free not only to buy pears and visit pubs and restaurants, but even – though they were advised against it – to discuss the trial with family and friends, and to read what the papers had to say on it. That had been the practice in England for ten years: and yet anarchy and disgrace had not descended there upon the practice of law and the quest for justice.

An alternative course of argument and action for Porter and Black might have been to agree with Lord Chief Justice Andrews that Taylor had been found guilty of a brutal and callous murder 'upon not merely convincing but conclusive evidence'; to show that on close consideration the irregularities in the conduct of the jurors and their keepers had done absolutely nothing to cast doubt on the correctness of the guilty verdict; and to indicate that an inquiry into these irregularities should be undertaken with a view to punishing any person or persons responsible for them and ensuring that the like would never happen again. Andrews in his submission had touched on the issue of responsibility and punishment, saying that 'even if the jurors or bailiffs fall short of what is required of them and become liable to penalties, the verdict may stand'; but that thought was quickly swept under the mental carpet. No such inquiry took place, no one was reprimanded or punished; the appeal judges' authoritative pronouncement that it was all an unfortunate accident had to be sustained.

22

FROM CONTEMPORARY NEWSPAPERS, court records, law reports, law journals; from the memories of women and men who lived in Belfast at the time and were in one way or another close to events; from letters, telephone calls, visits; from conversations with some who are willing to be named and some (like the 'Gibbonses') who prefer not: that is how this story has been put together. Sometimes a missing piece of the jigsaw turned up most unexpectedly, a chance recollection strengthening a reasonable explanation.

The suggestion here is that in all likelihood the second trial was deliberately sabotaged (becoming in the end 'a vain and useless ceremonial', 'an affront to the dignity of justice') and that the appeal judges and perhaps a few of the other lawyers and lawyer-politicians involved realised that. To reinforce this claim, let us return to the problem of Robert's baffling display of cheerful indifference when he came into court to face the almost certain verdict of guilty and the sentence of death, a performance so strikingly unlike his conduct at the end of the first trial. A conversation between Gerald Dowd and a certain Douglas Edwards would seem to resolve this problem.

'Dougie' Edwards hailed from Derby and served in the British army during the war. He was stationed in Northern Ireland, where he met and married a local girl. After demobilisation, he found employment in the Northern Ireland Prison Service; but having been denied overseas service during the war, he felt he would like to see something of the wide world, so that after five years as a prison warder he joined the King's African Police and was sent to Kenya. He paid dearly for his wanderlust. When Mau-Mau resistance to British rule broke out he was involved in a violent confrontation with some rebels and had his wrists slashed, permanently losing normal dexterity in one hand. Thus incapacitated, he returned to Belfast with his wife during the late 1960s and found work as a 'runner' in the old law firm of Lestrange and Bretton, his job being to perform such menial tasks as delivering letters and stamping deeds. But he was a cheerful stoic, 'a character', and also intelligent: despite his handicap, he took up study by night, got three A-levels and signed on for an extern degree. Not surprisingly, he was respected and befriended by some of the young solicitors in the firm. One of these was Gerald Dowd.

Over a pint in Mooney's round the corner from their office in Chichester Street, Gerald and Dougie fell to talking one day about odd court cases. Gerald mentioned the Taylor case as the strangest he had heard of and explained that he knew the murdered woman and had lived in the Newington area himself. Dougie capped this by saying that he had got to know Taylor quite well. He had been one of three warders assigned the task of watching over him during the two months he was in the condemned cell awaiting the outcome of the appeal. Dougie had to listen without comment to Taylor's compulsive monologues – about his hard life, treacherous friends, Catholics, 'stupid fuckin' judges', sex, luck, winning and losing – and what he was going to do when he got out of 'this place'. Said Dougie:

> He was a cocky little bastard. I really disliked him,
> but of course I couldn't show it. One thing he kept on
> saying – and he was right in the end – was, 'They're
> not going to hang *me*. No sir!' He knew. *He knew.*

Given the unpredictability of legal outcomes, it was undoubtedly foolish of Robert to place such complete faith in the assurances he must have been given. But it was characteristic too: it fitted with the recklessness of the gambler convinced that luck was once more on his side. Which it surely was.

23

AROUND NOON ON THE DAY of Robert Taylor's release, Mrs Kate Hale was standing on top of her treadle sewing machine in the bay window of her house on Cliftonpark Avenue, adjacent to the rear entrance to the Gaol. She was hanging up a new set of curtains she had made, but was distracted by the sight of two men passing by on the empty street almost immediately below her. The smaller one was talking animatedly and she realised from his boyish looks, blue suit and white open-necked shirt who he was. Like everyone else, she had followed the story in the papers and knew that the appeal judgment was being delivered that morning. 'He was carrying a small brown paper parcel under his arm. I got quite a shock, I can tell you!' she said to Mrs Benson, her next-door neighbour. A few minutes later, she noticed that the other man turned back. She did not know that his name was Edwards, nor could she see him disappear into the Gaol by way of the gate door from which the two had emerged. But she was armed with a morsel of Belfast history that would enliven her neighbourly chats ever after.

Robert had not been in court to hear the judgment, but his father and some of his father's friends were there, as well as a host of other well-wishers from the Bay. When Porter announced his verdict of acquittal, the usual buzz of talk and shuffling of feet began. But a court crier surprised everyone by calling loudly for silence – Hanna was approaching the judges. He came, he said, to discuss costs:

> Your Lordships, may I respectfully remind you that
> the appellant is entirely without means. He received a
> certificate in the first trial. The second was paid for.
> But in this appeal – the outlay for which I have al-
> ready submitted – nothing has been received.

'We are sorry, Mr Hanna,' said Porter, as he and his colleague turned to go. 'I am afraid we are unable to help the appellant in that matter.' And that was that. They had done enough
for the appellant already and, unless Robert senior's Men In The
Know could help again, Hanna would have to shoulder the costs
himself: a not unfair return, however, for his sweeping victory
in Duncairn Ward, which would in turn be a stepping stone to
much higher things.

Hardly anyone except those at the press table heard this little exchange or noticed the triumphant Hanna's sudden look of
irritation. For the buzz resumed within seconds of the crier's call
and the court quickly emptied. In the main hall outside, Taylor's
supporters performed a kind of victory dance while some others
were shaking their heads and exchanging looks of disbelief. And
then a few minutes later, when the bewigged Hanna, Fox and
Lunn emerged from the courtroom, 'a small, white-haired man'
(said *The Irish News*) approached to thank and congratulate
them and to receive in return what one observer thought artifi-
cial smiles ('No smile in the eyes, you know'). Outside, a large
crowd made for the Gaol opposite, expecting to witness Taylor's walk to freedom through the door in the main gate. They
waited for well over half an hour, during which time several
people came out past the policemen on door duty. But no sign of
Robert. Then the great doors were opened and a horse-drawn
cart heaped with laundry bags emerged: 'He's in one of those!'
shouted a wag, and everyone laughed. Eventually they were told
that Taylor had already left and would be home by now. After
some indignant outbursts, the Tiger's Bay folk went off together

in noisy good humour. Someone in front hoisted the Union Jack, someone else struck up 'The Sash' and the others joined in. They marched back to the Bay via Eia Street and the top of Duncairn Gardens, where they jeered and gesticulated across at Ponsonby, visible through a great gap left by the bombings of 1941. There would be powerful craic tonight in Morrison's, a great weekend in fact. Extra police remained on duty all night in certain districts of the city, but no trouble attended the bonfires and dancing that enlivened Tiger's Bay long after closing time.

In a smooth operation, obviously thought out in advance of the verdict, the authorities had managed to avoid the extreme embarrassment of a well-photographed theatrical scene in which a callous murderer was set at liberty by the Northern Ireland judiciary, to be greeted as a hero on his escape from captivity. As soon as Porter uttered the word 'acquittal', Captain T.D. Morrison, Belfast Commissioner of Police, went to the telephone and called the Governor of the Gaol, upon which Robert was instructed to prepare for a quiet exit by the back door of the building. It was not entirely quiet. As he was escorted by Edwards from the condemned cell down the corridors whose tarred strips had fed his imagination, there were cries from the cells:

'Third time lucky, eh?'

'What about me, pretty boy? I got three years for next to nothin'!'

'Hey, lad, d'ya think Geordie Hanna could work miracles for me?'

'Good luck, Bobby, you're gonna need it.'

The plan of the authorities was not designed with Robert's comfort in mind, but it coincided with his own and his father's wishes: if his luck was to last, he would have to lie low and keep his picture out of the papers.

Once parted from Edwards, he followed a slightly circuitous route back to Number 13, a distance of little over a mile: from

Cliftonpark Avenue to Cliftonville Road, then across Halliday's Road on to Hillman Street and back home by way of Norman Street. Number 13 was situated at the corner where Norman and Meadow Street conjoin, so that he arrived at his house behind the crowd of well-wishers, journalists and photographers who were looking up Meadow Street in expectation that he would be driven down there in a taxi, as his father had done shortly before. They did not notice him turn the corner behind them. He was almost into the house before he was spotted. According to *The Irish Press*, when they saw him, the crowd (mostly women) instantly began to sing:

> For he's a jolly good fellow,
> He's a jolly good fellow,
> He's a jolly good feh-eh-low,
> And so say all of us.
> And so say all of us . . .

The men from *The Irish News* and the *Irish Press* described the homecoming non-committally. But the Unionist papers did not. *The News-Letter* spoke of 'moving scenes' at the Taylor home and the *Belfast Telegraph*, in addition to its long summary of the appeal ruling, devoted a separate piece to The Return. Here no thought of a judicial farce and the slaughter of a good woman disturbed a narrative whose manner vaguely recalled centuries-old stories of the long-lost hero's return and his joyful reunion with kith and kin in an emotional experience shared by the whole community. 'Reunion of Taylor Family – the First Since Easter', 'Ordeal Was Over', went its captions. It told how 'the boyish figure' of Taylor 'with a small parcel under his arm, unobtrusively' – as if modestly – 'slipped past the crowd' and entered his house. It told how 'the news that Taylor was free swept through the city like wildfire'; how 'people stood in groups in Meadow Street, Brougham Street, Duncairn Gardens

and York Street discussing the event'; how they were heard saying, 'His mother wept for joy' and 'I wonder what he will do
now'. A *rite de passage*, it seemed, had been accomplished. No
one knows better than the citizens of Belfast that there is always
more than one way of telling the same story – now as then.

*

For some, this is where the story of Robert the Painter properly
ends, its significance exhausted; they might reasonably close
here and assume they will miss nothing of consequence in doing
so. But for others, questions will remain about the afterlives of
the chief participants; and the answers to those questions throw
a little more light on the strangeness of human nature, on the
nature of Northern Ireland and on the unfinished story of its
chronic Troubles.

24

THE APPEAL JUDGMENT GIVEN, the case closed, what would
the twenty-one-year-old hero do now? What would the
twenty-one-year-old daughter of the woman he murdered do?
Where would they go, what became of them, how would they
cope with the effects of an experience which in different ways
had utterly transformed their lives? Did Kathleen spend the rest
of her days in a dark bitterness at the injustice of it all, matching
the dark guilt in which Robert would be forever enclosed? And
what of the lawyers and lawyer-politicians – Porter, Hanna,
Lunn, Curran and Warnock – who figured so conspicuously in
the lives of these two young people? Symbols of the Establishment, they deserve at least an appendix, which I have granted
them; one of them – Curran – has already figured in a memorable novel which troubles the historically minded with its bold

mixture of fiction and fact, and intrigues others with its stylistic
bravura and topographical errors.

Robert has spent a lifetime seeking invisibility, and with considerable success. Characteristically, however, he took risks at the
start. On 22 February 1950 he was seen by reporters making Lily
a respectable woman at the Register Office near the city centre
(his parents attended; hers did not). As noted earlier, however, his
luck held and he managed to frustrate the efforts of *The Belfast
Telegraph*'s photographer to provide the public with an identifiable face for the boyish killer. But a few days later, James Kelly,
northern editor of the Dublin *Independent*, was in the Belfast office of the London *Daily Mail* talking to its resident editor when
(he writes me) 'who should walk in but Taylor and his unlovely
wife! They had come to offer their story for a fair price.' The offer was declined. Not long after this, Kelly was walking past
Queen's Arcade in the city centre with his mother when he turned
and said to her: 'Do you see this fellow coming towards us, bold
as brass? That's the man who murdered Mrs McGowan and got
off on a flimsy technicality.' 'She was shocked,' he says. But she
was not nearly so shocked as was Kathleen McGowan when, one
chilly morning in mid-March, she realised who was sitting in
front of her on the Antrim Road tram, chatting cheerfully to his
companion. She got off immediately and walked home, feeling
sick. How could she stay in this place?

At first, he himself fully intended to stay. He did not return
to his old occupation, however, for the name of 'Robert the
Painter' was one he desperately wanted to erase from history.
Through his father's connections, he found employment in
McHugh Dick's, a wood supply and carpentry firm; Archie
Williamson (son of the Williamson who agreed to his postponed
taxi-and-carnation payment) says that according to a senior em-
ployee of that firm he was 'a good reliable worker and a decent
lad – whatever the other lot said about him'. But after being

attacked by one of the other lot outside his old haunt, The Deer's Head, he tried to emigrate to Australia and was refused entry. Then there were rumours that he went to Canada and in the early 1970s that he had died there of cancer; and then again that he had died in England. After that there were no more rumours. In the mayhem of the '70s, '80s and '90s, what did his crime and non-punishment matter? Who now cared?

His name came to public notice again in 2000, by which time he would have been – or was – seventy-two. In the 30 July issue of Belfast's populist *Sunday World*, Hugh Jordan, a Scotsman recently settled in the city, wrote an article which was printed with an extra-large, eye-grabbing caption placed to the left of a picture of a pub in Donaghadee:

DEAD

THE KILLER WHO
ESCAPED DEATH
PENALTY BECAUSE
JURY GOT DRUNK

If Robert had been alive he could not have asked for a more decisive blow to any suspicion that he was still enjoying his ill-gotten freedom. And whether he was dead or alive, the Ulster Establishment would have been quite pleased with the way in which his story was told. After reporting that 'he died . . . in Canada last week' (specific location and date not mentioned), the article devoted all its attention to the crime, the two trials and the reason why the guilty man got off. The slant of the narrative may have had something to do with the way the story of 'Robert the Painter' has come to be told in Belfast folklore, a piece of craic in the pubs; or it may have been suggested to Jordan by the individual who (he says) phoned him up from foreign parts with news of Taylor's death and suggested it would be a

good occasion for a lively article. The following sentences – the
italics are Jordan's – encapsulate the spin:

> However, instead of settling for a seafront stroll they
> took a coach to Donaghadee where they went drink-
> ing in the famous Grace Neill's bar . . .

> A few of the jury went for a walk, but the majority
> headed for Grace Neill's bar where they boozed the
> night away discussing the day's proceedings in court
> with the locals . . .

> The night after their Donaghadee outing they took a
> trip to Antrim – without the court's permission – and
> hit the bars there . . .

> *And the more drunk they got the more they talked*
> *about the murder case . . .*

> Lord Justice Porter was clearly shocked . . . he told
> Taylor he was free to leave the court. Two days later,
> without saying a word about the case, Robert Taylor
> quit Belfast for Canada where he started a new life,
> and he died peacefully in his bed last week.

What had seemed to some to be a shocking tale of justice
mocked and law subverted had become a mad Irish farce, an
essentially innocent spree with a happy ending; a subject which
might have attracted the author of *The Playboy of the Western
World*. On the day after the publication of the article, both *The
Irish News* and *The Belfast Telegraph* printed short items announcing Taylor's death 'in Canada' (specific date and location
again not mentioned) and recalling the story in brief and without
factual errors; the precise date and the particular location in
Canada were unmentioned for the simple reason (privately con-

fessed) that the papers' source for this piece of Irish news was the resident Scotsman's article.

The factual errors in Jordan's comical narrative, his ignorance of just where in Canada Taylor had allegedly lived and died, and the elusiveness of his phone-caller ('on a world cruise at the time') prompted one sceptical reader to put it to him that Taylor was not dead and that he had been set up to write the story. If Taylor were still alive in 2000, he and his protectors would have noted with some apprehension the proposal of the Director of Public Prosecutions in England, broadcast on the BBC and discussed in the newspapers from January onwards, to change the so-called double jeopardy rule, the law which means that a suspect cannot be tried twice for the same crime if he has been acquitted of an offence based on the same facts. Retrials, said the DPP, should be possible 'in exceptional cases' – 'we have had examples in recent war crimes cases when it has been possible to try an accused for an offence committed over fifty years ago.' This proposal (which has since become law) was prompted by public outrage at the spectacle of the alleged racist murderers of Stephen Lawrence brazenly walking the streets of London.

Whatever about the double jeopardy explanation, Jordan agreed that he might have been set up to announce a fictitious death, for a few days after the publication of his article an old Belfast detective whom he knew phoned him to say that it was well known in police circles that Taylor had been back in North Belfast for years. And indeed he was. What better place and time to hide in than Tiger's Bay in the late '70s and Rathcoole – the new Loyalist enclave further out – in the '80s and '90s? There his past shocked no one; the walls of hatred and fear which encircled those communities were his security; murder was commonplace. He lived and maybe still lives among men whose sectarian killings have brought them local renown, jolly good fellows all. His only trouble has been with the local children, who heard jocular whisperings at home. When he would emerge each week to collect his pension, now a replica of his father, the slight grey-haired man mentioned by reporters at the trials, they would sometimes dare to follow him at a distance, chanting, 'Robert the Painter! Robert the Painter! Robert the Painter!' He would not tell them that names, unlike sticks and stones, will break no bones. He would turn quickly and glare at them, eyes narrowed, teeth clenched; and his look – if looks could – would kill. Thus far had he come from the days of his innocence when in Ponsonby he winked at the young girls and they laughed and ran away, pleased.

25

OF ALL THE WITNESSES CONSULTED in the writing of this story, the most elusive, the most surprising and the last to be found was Kathleen McGowan. My encounter with her subtly challenged my whole perception of a story that had haunted me ever since I left my native city of Belfast (and Ireland) for good in the 1950s. At this ending point, therefore, I may perhaps be permitted to enter the narrative myself.

In search of Kathleen, I first consulted a small friendship group, consisting of retired lawyers, teachers and businessmen, who call themselves The Newingtonians; they live scattered and far from the old place, but meet monthly for lunch in a Belfast restaurant. One of them had met Kathleen by chance on the Strand in London in 1970, but that was the last that any of these old men had heard of her; they thought she might be dead by now. More than a year later, however, I was directed by one of the surviving Casey sisters to Nancy Sherry, a contemporary of Kathleen's who still lived in Newington and was thought to be a likely source of information; which she was. She gave me Kathleen's address in England, I wrote to her and received a prompt and friendly reply. A few months later, I made my way down from my home in Yorkshire to visit her in the small south-coast resort where she lived.

On a hot day in July 2003, I checked in for the night in a seafront hotel named after one of England's stateliest homes. It had seen better days and so had the town. The effects of cheap package holidays abroad were evident everywhere. A faded *For Sale* notice was affixed to a huge empty building that was once the town's most opulent hotel. Cheap eating places and take-aways abounded, a good restaurant was impossible to find; shoddy amusement arcades were everywhere. But there were signs of elegance and care still on the Edwardian avenues in the residential district high above the town where Kathleen lived. Her own house, however, as she had forewarned me on the tele-phone, stood out unkindly from the rest: faded and peeling paint, cracked woodwork, an overgrown garden; twenty years' neglect and all the sadness of time passing.

She had told me to push the front door open and knock on the dining-room door on the right as I came in. She was, she had explained, permanently confined to that room now; it was her bedroom and her sitting room. She had a weak heart and suf-fered acutely from diabetes; arthritis in both knees was so severe that she could move only with the greatest difficulty and with the help of two sticks.

The front door was indeed ajar. I made my way past a bicy-cle in the hall and saw at the end of the corridor the hesitant fig-ure of a middle-aged man, who withdrew shyly into the shadows of the kitchen; it was Alan, her brain-damaged son, who lived alone with her. I knocked on the dining-room door and heard her move slowly across the room to open it. She leaned heavily on two sticks and looked up at me with large brown eyes that sparkled with life and interest.

She sat on the white counterpane of the bed and insisted that I take the only chair. It seemed to me for a moment that all her possessions and memories were contracted into that faded room: a mantelpiece and walls packed with pictures and family photographs; bulging bookcases; a piano stacked with more books and more photographs; a china cabinet capped with mementos and knick-knacks; a little table with sherry and two glasses at the ready; a tray stand with china and a plate of neatly cut sandwiches below a pure white napkin; hardly an inch to move.

She greeted me with a warmth and talked with a readiness and enthusiasm that took me greatly by surprise. There was no heaviness in her voice or countenance. It was apparent that in her mind she had somehow drawn a line round the tragedy of 1949–50; that although she had never returned to Belfast she still remembered her life outside those nine months with great affection and longed to talk about it and her old friends. Did I know anything about the Caseys, the Dowds, the Cassidys, the Raffertys, the Slevins, the Cunnings? Had I spoken to so-and-so and so-and-so?

She told me that she had felt utterly desolate when her father died. When her mother was killed she was the object of everyone's concern, sustained by a huge sympathy; but it was inevitably very different when, without brother or sister to share her grief, she sat alone by her father's bed in Ponsonby Avenue and watched him die. Much of her happiness in Belfast had been tied up with the Group Theatre, where she studied acting, and so her departure for the Guildhall School of Music and Drama in London seemed to her the one way back into life. And it was. She finished her diploma, made many new friends and fell in love. But marriage to John Woodhouse and a large family precluded an acting career. However, she retained an intense interest in the theatre and virtually all her books, collected for her by her lawyer husband, related to the stage – play texts, theatre history, biographies of the great actors and actresses. She was reading a life of the Victorian actress Fanny Kemble when I arrived – still the daughter of the apprentice barman who loved the theatre and took lessons in elocution.

Her large family was consolation for someone who had been an only child, left an orphan. But there was sadness and even tragedy here too. A child died in infancy. A much-loved son died in his twenties. Alan had been deprived of oxygen at birth and suffered brain damage in consequence ('We look after each other,' she said wistfully). Serious illness forced her husband to retire in middle age and they had to leave their lovely home; he died a few years later. She had caring daughters and grandchildren, but they lived at a distance. One might think that all of this, added to her early experience of misery, would have given her a gloomy or embittered outlook. But not so: she seemed to dwell only on the good things in her life; she wanted to talk about her daughters' achievements, about actors past and present, and about current events (she was 'sorry for that poor man Trimble' then trying in vain to negotiate between extremes). She smiled and laughed easily. Battered in the past, ill and incapacitated in the present, she retained an indestructible spirit of life and a radical human-kindness that shone in her eyes and animated her voice. Had she completely transcended the tyrannous claims of the past, I wondered, might she inspire one to join those who still held out hopes for true peace and reconciliation in Northern Ireland?

Although she shared with me many of her happy memories of people and events in Belfast and filled in many gaps in my knowledge of Taylor and his trials, clearly she had no strong desire to talk about the events with which in time I had come to identify her almost completely; there seemed to be no stored up intensity of feeling waiting for any sympathetic ear. But she did not hesitate to talk about the tragedy, even its most poignant details. She showed me the mother-of-pearl rosary beads, her father's copy of *Bell's Elocution Reader*, photographs of that farmhouse under the Down mountains that she loved so much. She recalled her mother's sadly misguided premonition about her uncle's fate and talked with great affection of the kindness shown to her by the Caseys. But I wanted to know just how the tragedy had affected her for the rest of her life. How, for example, did she explain it to her children?

'Oh, I never told them.'

I wondered if I had heard her aright: 'You never told them!'

'No. Not until you wrote to me last month. Life is difficult enough for young people growing up. Then when you wrote to me, I thought the time had come and I told them.'

Then I asked the one question that had always been uppermost in my mind: how did she feel when Taylor got off? How deep and how lasting was her sense of injustice?

'Well, some of my friends were very angry with me for this,' she said, 'but every day during the appeal I went round to the church and prayed that it would succeed and he would not be hanged. I was so relieved when it did.'

'But why? Why?'

'Oh, I just couldn't carry the thought of two horrible deaths in my mind for the rest of my life. I felt that if they didn't hang him I might be able to start a new life.'

I looked at her for a while and then said:

'He was exactly the same age as you, I remember, three years older than me. He might be alive still. If you met him now, how would you feel?'

(With a little nervous laugh) 'Oh, I'd be frightened.'

'Would you forgive him?'

'If he sincerely asked forgiveness, yes.'

We had talked for three hours and I felt she must be tired. I rose to go and said I would call a taxi to take me back to town, as it was much too hot to walk, but she said, 'Let me', and with instant recall dialled a number. 'He's very good, this man,' she said, and then begged me to phone her now and then, just to talk to her about old times (the good ones) and the theatre. Which I did.

In the taxi, the driver seemed pleased to know that a compatriot had come to see her. 'I used to take her regularly into town every Saturday – before she became housebound. Now it's just once or twice to the hospital.'

'She's a nice lady,' he added.

And then, reflectively, a moment or two later:

'A very nice lady.'

EPILOGUE

Let us leave Kathleen in her serenity and return to 1950 to reflect in conclusion on a very different relationship between past and present.

One of the most remarkable features of Taylor's case is that when the appeal judges ruled that he had "by some unfortunate mischance" been denied justice, and so allowed him to return to the bosom of his family as a free man, the decision met with no adverse public comment, indeed no public comment of any kind. Even the editorial columns of *The Irish News*, so vocal on the wickedness of partition, gerrymandering and discrimination in the allocation of jobs and housing, had nothing to say. The silence of thoughtful Protestants may have been due to embarrassment. The silence of Catholics perhaps betokened a weary cynicism: "What else would you expect?" "When the Crowd Shouted They Let the Thief Escape".

Moreover, although it had riveted the attention of the divided Ulster community for more than six months in 1949–50, the case was never mentioned publicly in "the quiet years" that followed. Understandably, too, it vanished from general consciousness in the turmoil of the Troubles. Nevertheless, it can

now be seen as a singularly portentous omen of 1969, when Nationalist alienation from the state, the judiciary and the RUC
finally exploded in demands for justice and civil rights, only to
be met by Loyalist indignation (orchestrated by the roaring Reverend Ian Paisley), police partiality, burnings and evictions; followed in turn by the spawning of monsters, both green and orange – the PIRA, the UDA, the UVF, the RHC, the LVF, the
INLA, the real IRA. Uniquely, then, although it turned on the
fate of two socially insignificant individuals, the case of Robert
the Painter is a single episode which encapsulates in itself the
essential meaning of Northern Ireland's history from 1920 until
the start of the Troubles.

Appendix: The Lawyers

AFTER HIS ASTONISHING APPEAL judgment, Judge Porter continued in the even tenor of his professional life. Just as he troubled no one by recommending that an inquiry into the jury fiasco should be held, so no one upset his calm conviction that he had dealt expertly with a most difficult case. Some disquiet was felt among a few top lawyers and it was rumoured that they thought the rules governing the non-separation of the jury should be brought in line with those in England; but it was very quiet disquiet. The necessary change was not made until 1973, long after Judge Porter had passed away (1956); nothing was done to raise unseemly questions about his forensic wisdom. After his death, he was accorded a splendid eulogy in *The Northern Ireland Legal Quarterly*, where the respect and affection in which he was held by his colleagues was registered with manifest sincerity. No mention was made in this eulogy of the laborious analysis which led him to the conclusion that a proven murderer should go free.

George Hanna's faithful servitor, 'wee Anthony Lunn', diligent collector of all those affidavits, was soon rewarded with the solicitor's plum job of Belfast Resident Magistrate.

Three years after he entered Stormont, Hanna shot to the top, being given responsibility for justice, law and order in Ulster as its Minister of Home Affairs. As such, he was quickly put to the test in the famous Longstone Road affair. Like the recent (post-1996) eruptions at Drumcree in County Armagh, this was a particularly troublesome manifestation of the Dolly's Brae Syndrome, the right of Orangemen to march through a Catholic district in (as Nationalists see it) an assertion of Loyalist supremacy. More immediately, the Longstone marches were symptomatic of Loyalist anger at the Anti-Partition campaign and the Unionist Government's 'appeasement' of Catholics in the new education arrangements of 1949; they were intended (in the words of the then MP for County Antrim, Nat Minford) to remind Catholics that 'Ulster is a Protestant country' and that Stormont 'is a Protestant parliament for a Protestant people'.

Longstone had been a problem shortly before Hanna came to office. In June 1952 Orangemen in Annalong, County Down, decided to march over Longstone Hill, a Catholic area which required a detour from their customary route. The Minister of Home Affairs, Brian Maginess, having already banned Nationalist marches in the centre of Enniskillen and Derry (largely Nationalist towns), was obliged to ban this march too. Such, however, was the indignation of the Orangemen that he backed down and gave permission to a different lodge to march along Longstone Road in July. But because local Catholics blocked the route and because the RUC had insufficient men to force a way through, the police kept the marchers at bay. This time the indignation of the Orangemen was province-wide and caused Prime Minister Brooke to move Maginess out of Home Affairs and instal George Hanna in his place. How would Hanna deal with this kind of conflict between the law and supremacist politics, justice and power?

At first he stood resolutely for impartiality in the treatment of Catholics and Protestants in the matter of marches and demonstrations, renewing the ban on the Longstone march and declaring memorably:

> I am quite satisfied that, were I to ban a Republican
> or any other opposition procession or meeting in one

> part of the country and, not only to permit an Orange
> procession in a Nationalist district, but to provide po-
> lice protection for that procession, I would be holding
> our entire administration up to ridicule and contempt.

Unfortunately for the new minister, however, it was in the very nature of Ulster politics that ridicule and contempt were the price that had to be paid from time to time for the rewards of office and power. He too had to bow to Orange pressure. He lifted the ban and on 12 July 1955, 15,000 Orangemen marched twice along Longstone Road. The march was headed by Brian Faulkner, MP, future Minister of Home Affairs and future Prime Minister, who on this occasion showed two of his prime-ministerial successors, James Chichester-Clarke and David Trimble, that a willingness to lead an Orange march in defiance of Government wishes could be the route to the highest office in Government. But Hanna's initial, outspoken opposition to the march lost him much favour with the Orange Order and, whether for that or other reasons, he never went further up the ladder of ambition. He withdrew from politics in 1956 to become a County Court Judge in County Down, in which role he would have to deal impartially with the misdemeanours of marchers and anti-marchers alike.

A few months before he rose to become Minister of Home Affairs, his career had interlocked with those of his former legal opponents and fellow Unionist MPs, Curran and Warnock, in a trial which would again bear witness to the strange workings of the law in the Six Counties of Ulster, proving to be both analogous and (in the person of Lancelot Curran) connected to the trial of Robert Taylor. This time all three of these members of the Establishment were very much on the same side, Hanna being Attorney General Warnock's junior counsel in the prosecution of Iain Hay Gordon, a twenty-year-old RAF technician accused of murdering Curran's daughter, Patricia, on 13 Novem-

ber 1952. The impression given by this legal set-up of unhealth-
ily close relationships in a tightly knit Establishment (where
change resembled a game of musical chairs or hat swapping)
was intensified by other considerations. The judge in the case,
Lord Chief Justice MacDermott, was a family friend of the Currans. The Inspector General of the RUC, Sir Richard Pim, who
also became involved in the case, was a close associate of
Curran. Moreover, the man accused of killing Curran's daughter
had great difficulty in finding anyone to defend him, and the
barristers who agreed to do so, Basil Kelly and H.A. McVeigh
QC (golfing partners of Curran), allegedly and understandably
did so on condition that they would not have to cross-examine
the Curran family.

Gordon was found guilty of the murder and only escaped
the hangman because his defence team went for and secured a
verdict of guilty but insane. Gordon thus spent seven years in
Holywell Asylum in County Antrim, where his sanity was apparent to everyone. The asylum's medical superintendent, Dr
Gilbert Smith, examined him on many occasions and found no
signs of mental abnormality, a judgement reinforced by forensic
psychiatrists who examined him prior to his successful appeal
hearing in 2000.

After their success in this high-profile case, Gordon's lawyers
went on to distinguish themselves in their profession, both becoming final arbiters in the most difficult cases presented to the
Northern Ireland judiciary. In 1965 McVeigh was made a Lord
Justice of Appeal, his co-partner in this being Lancelot Curran
(who had earlier succeeded Porter and joined Black in that office). Kelly became a Unionist MP and Attorney General as well
as Lord Justice of Appeal, leaving the latter office some five or
six years before Gordon's case finally emerged from the distant
past to pose extremely difficult questions for the Court of Appeal.
With a room named after him in the Institute of Professional

Legal Studies in Queen's University, Belfast, Sir Basil is now one of the most esteemed members of his profession in the North.

The young man whom he helped to save from the gallows was naive, timid, physically frail and without a trace of Robert Taylor's resilience and cunning. He was subjected to harsh and sustained interrogation by the police; and although he insisted at first that he was innocent, he eventually broke down and signed a very curious confession, one which suggests that the idea of pleading guilty but insane originated on the prosecution side. In this statement, he admitted murdering the girl but indicated repeatedly that he was unaware of what he was doing and was still quite uncertain as to what exactly happened:

> I probably pulled the body through the bushes to hide it . . . I dragged her by her arms or hands, but I cannot remember. . . . I was confused at the time and believe I stabbed her. . . . It is all very hazy to me. . . . I must have remained hidden. . . . As far as I know . . . I felt that something awful must have happened. . . . I must have done this but I do not quite remember. . . . He may have said . . . I just cannot remember.

He signed for several reasons: because he was exhausted, hungry and desperate for his ordeal to end after ten-hour sessions in which four policemen kept up a continuous barrage of accusatory demands: 'We know you're guilty! Confess it!'; because he had no solicitor or RAF officer to stand by him at any time during the interrogation sessions; and because John Capstick, the tough detective brought over from Scotland Yard to head the inquiry, focused insistently and improperly on his homosexual encounters and warned – to Gordon's horror – that his devout Christian parents would learn about these; and finally, because he was led to believe that, if he did sign, his homosexual associations would not be made public and he would soon be free.

He quickly retracted this confession, explaining to his lawyers the nature and extent of the pressure which was brought to
bear on him, and the fact that he had not dictated the confession
but that it was devised by Capstick through a question and answer method. On these grounds, before the jury entered and the
trial proper began, the defence argued with Judge MacDermott
that the confession should not be admitted. The irregularities in
the manner of conducting the interrogation, together with the
style of the statement (indicating a carefully composed narrative
into which a broken and confused person might allow himself to
be pushed), should have been enough for any wise judge to
deem the confession inadmissible. In a lecture on 'The Quality
of Judgment' delivered to students of the Northern Ireland Inn
of Court in 1969, Lord MacDermott would extol the attribute of
judgment and describe it as 'a sort of forensic wisdom which is
supported by, rather than derived from, a knowledge of the law
and the facts of the given case' (*Northern Ireland Legal Quarterly*, 21 [1970] 179). Some forty-seven years after the trial one
of his distinguished successors would find that, in the Gordon
case, the forensic wisdom of the good judge deserted him when
he ruled that the accused's confession was admissible. By doing
so, he in effect sealed Gordon's fate as the alleged murderer of
his friend's daughter and ensured that no one else would be
brought under suspicion; his ruling indicated to the defence that
the only hope for their client was to accept Captick's intimation
that Gordon was not sane – that he did not know (as Capstick
'knew') what he was doing when the murder 'happened'.

But even apart from the confession, the case against Gordon
had a number of important weaknesses. Some of these, moreover, carried ominous suggestions of an attempt to pin the blame
on him (but not at the cost of his life) so as to prevent the investigation moving along a very dark path into socially and politi-
cally dangerous territory.

Judge Curran's daughter was allegedly attacked at about 5.45 pm halfway up the long dark drive to Glen House, the family home in Whiteabbey on the outskirts of Belfast, her body being left by the killer in shrubbery some forty feet from the driveway. According to the forensic pathologist brought over from England (our old friend Dr Firth), she must have been carried to the spot where she was found, since there were no signs of drag marks either on the ground or on her clothing. But Gordon's confession says that he dragged her off the driveway; furthermore, it seems unlikely that a slender young man could have lifted and carried an inert body weighing over nine stone (Capstick obviously realised this when he specified 'dragging' and 'pulling' in the statement).

More importantly, however, Firth pointed out that Patricia's wounds were so severe (she had been stabbed thirty-seven times, her heart was pierced twice and the arteries in both her legs were severed) that both the person who carried her and the ground where she was left would have been saturated with blood. But only three small spots of blood were found on leaves near the body. This suggests that she was not murdered on or near the driveway and that she had been carried there some time after the crime took place. Furthermore, no trace of blood from Patricia's blood group was found on Gordon's clothing. Nor was there any sign that he had just completed a singularly bloody murder (at 5.45 pm) when he was seen by fellow serviceman James Spence entering the NAAFI canteen at 6.00 pm. Spence's statement to this effect, not disclosed to the defence team, came to light as a result of journalist John Linklater's investigations in the 1990s and was noted in the report made by the Criminal Review Commission in 2000. It was kept secret by the police because in a second interview of four hours' duration Spence, not realising the full import of this change, eventually agreed with the police that he could only have seen Gordon in the canteen at 7.00 pm – a change which Spence subsequently regretted and ascribed to police pressurising. Interviewed by a *Sunday Life* reporter in October 2000, Spence said Gordon was an 'odd' and 'nervous' sort and the butt of jokes at the RAF base, but 'honest' and definitely 'not capable of such a thing. Just not up to it'. He expressed his amazement that his first statements were not given by the police to the defence lawyers. 'My evidence might have made all the difference,' he said.

The portfolio of books which Patricia carried with her on her return from university was found, together with her handbag and woollen hat, at the edge of the driveway adjacent to the body, neatly deposited and in a dry condition; this is not consistent with the claim that she was the victim of a violent assault at that point nor with the fact that it had been raining lightly for two hours before 5.45 pm, the time of the alleged attack. It suggests rather that the person or persons who left her body nearby lacked the presence of mind to arrange the pretended scene of the crime correctly; it suggests too that she was attacked indoors.

This brings us to the most disturbing aspect of the case, the behaviour of the Currans immediately before, and then after, the discovery of Patricia's body. At 1.35 am Judge Curran called the home of his family solicitor, Malcolm Davison. He told Mrs Davison that he had called other friends, the Steels, and learned from them that their son John had left Patricia to the 5.00 pm bus for Whiteabbey; he also asked Malcolm Davison to come to The Glen. At 1.45 am he phoned the local police station asking if there had been an accident involving a bus and informing them too that he had called some friends and learned that Patricia had left Belfast on the 5.00 pm bus. Constable Rutherford offered to come round to help in the search for Patricia but was told by the judge that that would not be necessary. At 1.50, however, a distraught Mrs Curran called the station, telling Rutherford that Patricia had travelled on the 5.00 pm bus and urging him to come round immediately, a request which would hardly have concurred with her husband's wishes. Rutherford and Davison reached the Glen at approximately 2.00 am, just when Curran and his son were on the point of discovering Patricia's body in the shrubbery.

Her legs were stiff, indicating that rigor mortis had begun. With some difficulty, the judge, his barrister son, Desmond, his solicitor and the policeman got her body into Davison's car and took it to the family doctor's home in Whiteabbey. It is strange, however, that four men of law should thus disturb the scene of a crime and handicap subsequent investigation. Desmond would claim (despite the apparent incipience of rigor mortis) that he thought he heard his sister breathe once when he came upon her; but if he and his father had thought there was any life left in the body, the most sensible, and surely too the most instinctive, action would have been to bring it to the house immediately and ask the doctor and an ambulance to come – not bundle it into a car and take it elsewhere.

Related to these oddities is evidence given to the police by the Steel family and the fact that this evidence was improperly withheld from the defence team, coming to public notice only as a result of Linklater's investigations. In their telephone calls at 1.35, 1.45 and 1.50 am, Curran and his wife said they had learned from friends (the Steels) that Patricia had travelled on the 5.00 pm bus from Belfast. But as the appeal judge reported in 2000, when John Steel and his parents were 'interviewed at length by the police, they were adamant . . . quite positive that it was not before 2.00 am' that they received the judge's call; they 'adhered very firmly to the time which they gave when the matter was [later] pursued with them by the police.' The inference is obvious: if the three Steels were correct about the time of the call they received, then Curran had learned from Patricia herself that she had come on the 5.00 pm bus; she was murdered after she came home and 'in some circumstances of which the Curran family were aware before they telephoned the Davisons' (Appeal Judgment, p. 32).

County Inspector Kennedy, who had interrogated Gordon, noted this contradiction, but as the appeal judge (Carswell LCJ) discreetly put it, he 'was reluctant to subject Mr Justice Curran or his wife to further distress by asking them to give evidence at the trial'; or as Kennedy himself wrote in his interim report, secret until recently, 'It was decided to pursue every line of inquiry before allowing our thoughts to concentrate on something which seemed too fantastic to believe, namely that the Currans were covering up the murder and telling a tissue of lies.' Soon after this decision, Desmond Curran pointed the finger of suspicion at Gordon (whom he had befriended at Church and brought home on two occasions); the Gordon line of inquiry was then energetically pursued and those who reflected on fantastic possibilities did so in private.

Kennedy was not the only person of importance involved in the case who noticed the conflict between what was stated by Judge Curran and by the Steels. Said the appeal judge:

> The contemporaneous notes of the Attorney General [i.e. Curran's friend Warnock, the prosecuting lawyer], whose handwriting is proved by . . . a document examiner, show that he also was alive to the discrepancy. The Crown [i.e. Warnock] nevertheless did not disclose the statements of Mr and Mrs Steel or that part of John Steel's statements which related to the time of the call from Mr Justice Curran.

Just as he was not questioned by the police, just as the police accepted his refusal to let them question his family until four days after the murder, and his refusal to let them conduct an examination of his house until a full week after the crime, so too he was, in effect, protected from the finger of suspicion by the prosecution lawyers and the judge. Moreover, Establishment determination to avoid embarrassing him was apparent much later. When Gordon was released from the asylum in 1960, Brian Faulkner, then Minister of Home Affairs, arranged for him to be flown home immediately and in secret to Glasgow under the name of John Cameron, his release being conditional on his and his family's keeping his misfortunes a secret. Ten years later, Prime Minister James Chichester-Clark successfully intervened with the BBC so as to suppress a Ludovic Kennedy documentary dealing with the case as a miscarriage of justice. Basil Kelly was the Ulster government's Attorney General at that time.

Curran's son Desmond was a quiet and deeply religious young man with an evangelising tendency that would lead him to abandon the law and spend the rest of his life as a missionary among the poor of a South African township. It was in order to share with Gordon his beliefs as a member of the Moral Rearmament Movement that he took the unusual step of inviting this awkward and unprepossessing twenty-year-old to dine with him and his family. The RAF technician felt socially out of his depth and (as he explained in a *Guardian* interview in November 2000) he found the atmosphere in the Curran home very strange. 'Patricia,' he said, 'was the only one who spoke to me. Desmond introduced me to his father – he just looked up from his newspaper and never spoke to me. It was like something from Victorian times – frigid and rigid. His mother was like a hen on hot bricks. I've never seen anything like her.'

Doris Curran may have seen Gordon as a potential addition to her unconventional daughter's list of unsuitable men friends. She had quarrelled with her on that subject, on her late nights and on her decision to take a summer job driving a builder's van; as she had quarrelled with her husband about his gambling debts. After the murder, she became a recluse and died a broken woman in 1975. The judge's domestic manner as described by Gordon accords with the fact that he never once spoke to Kathleen McGowan during either of the two trials in which she had to provide such painful testimony. However, his mysterious conduct during the murder investigation (which he assuredly would have known would invite the suspicion that he was engaged in a cover-up) did not affect his professional career adversely. In 1956 he became Lord Justice of Appeal in that Supreme Court which much later would overturn the verdict on Gordon; and he was knighted in 1964. But he became more remote than ever. A colleague, Richard Ferguson QC, described him in these later years as 'a cold, aloof figure who carried a tremendous sorrow'. Was that because of his daughter's death, or because he had been guilty of a profound betrayal of everything he stood for? At any rate, the High Court Judge who obstructed the investigation into his daughter's murder bore no moral resemblance to the brilliant advocate whose icy questions and resolute pursuit of truth exposed the guilt of Robert Taylor for all to see.

Desmond's conversion to Catholicism was another source of alienation for the judge; it seemed like a calculated affront to his Presbyterian and Loyalist selfhood. Desmond was banned from the family home after his conversion and lived for several months with a Catholic family, the Sherrys, in Atlantic Avenue; Michael Sherry, another very religious young professional (an engineer), had met him in the ecumenically inclined Moral Rearmament Movement and was to some extent responsible for his conversion. Michael stoutly rejects any suggestion that responsibility for Patricia's death should be traced to her family, though his position on this does not accommodate the deeply puzzling aspects of the case. Reinforcing and complicating the strange link between Ulster's two most notorious murder cases, Michael introduced Desmond to his friend Kathleen McGowan, who found him a rather shy, charming and humble person; he was one of those who attended the melancholy farewell party she gave when she left Belfast forever. He too took the exile's path, leaving soon after that party to study abroad for the priesthood.

Five years later Desmond invited his father to attend his ordination ceremony in – of all places – Rome. To the surprise of everyone and the horror of many, Curran accepted the invitation, thereby effecting his automatic expulsion from the Orange Order. Did he feel it was a sacrifice he owed his son? Or was the path to Rome a thorny penance demanded by his Christian conscience?

After his return to Scotland, Iain Hay Gordon endured a kind of twilight existence and suffered continuously from nightmares of accusation and eternal confinement. When the appeal court dismissed the guilty verdict against him as unsound in 2000, he felt truly free for the first time in half a century. He was interviewed at the time by many journalists, all of whom expressed astonishment at his complete lack of bitterness against anyone – even against Desmond, who still declared him guilty. This freedom from bitterness was arguably a more redeeming feature of the case – one in which a young woman was violently done to death, the police, the judiciary and the state colluded in suppressing the truth, and a young man's life was blighted – than was Desmond's work as a priest among the dispossessed of South Africa.

Duncan Webb, an investigative journalist who wrote for *The People*, was for years obsessed with the mysteries of the Curran case, much as the author of this book has been haunted by the concealed truths and larger significance of the Taylor case (an Ulster parable, an omen of the Troubles). When after Judge Curran's death in 1984 Glen House was sold and the carpets lifted, he gained access to the house and found on the floorboards in one of the upstairs rooms a large, dark stain which he believed to be blood – Patricia's blood. But Webb died suddenly and his research was never published; moreover, forensic science might not have been sufficiently advanced at the time to evaluate his discovery. Rightly, no doubt, it was not mentioned in the submission to the Court of Appeal in 2000; but it lingers in the margins of history and in the mind's eye as a troubling image of its time and place.